my revision notes

WJEC Eduqas GCSE

PE

Ross Howitt

HODDER
EDUCATION
AN HACHETTE UK COMPANY

Acknowledgements

The Publishers would like to thank the following for permission to reproduce copyright material.

p.7 © anatols/iStock/Thinkstock; **p.8** © Ria Novosti/TopFoto; **p.49** © Blanaru/iStock/Thinkstock.

Every effort has been made to trace all copyright holders, but if any have been inadvertently overlooked, the Publishers will be pleased to make the necessary arrangements at the first opportunity.

Although every effort has been made to ensure that website addresses are correct at time of going to press, Hodder Education cannot be held responsible for the content of any website mentioned in this book. It is sometimes possible to find a relocated web page by typing in the address of the home page for a website in the URL window of your browser.

Hachette UK's policy is to use papers that are natural, renewable and recyclable products and made from wood grown in sustainable forests. The logging and manufacturing processes are expected to conform to the environmental regulations of the country of origin.

Orders: please contact Bookpoint Ltd, 130 Milton Park, Abingdon, Oxon OX14 4SE. Telephone: +44 (0)1235 827720. Fax: +44 (0)1235 400401. Email education@bookpoint.co.uk. Lines are open from 9 a.m. to 5 p.m., Monday to Saturday, with a 24-hour message answering service. You can also order through our website: www.hoddereducation.co.uk.

ISBN: 978 1 5104 2940 6

© Ross Howitt 2018

First published in 2018 by
Hodder Education,
An Hachette UK Company
Carmelite House
50 Victoria Embankment
London EC4Y 0DZ

www.hoddereducation.co.uk

Impression number		10	9	8	7	6	5	4	3	2
Year			2023	2022	2021	2020	2019	2018

Cover photo © Flashon Studio/123RF.com
Illustrations by Integra
Typeset by Bembo Std Regular 11/13 by Integra Software Services Pvt. Ltd., Pondicherry, India
Printed in Spain

A catalogue record for this title is available from the British Library.

Get the most from this book

Everyone has to decide his or her own revision strategy, but it is essential to review your work, learn it and test your understanding. These Revision Notes will help you to do that in a planned way, topic by topic. Use this book as the cornerstone of your revision and don't hesitate to write in it – personalise your notes and check your progress by ticking off each section as you revise.

Tick to track your progress

Use the revision planner on pages iv–vi to plan your revision, topic by topic. Tick each box when you have:

- revised and understood a topic
- tested yourself
- practised the exam questions and checked your answers.

You can also keep track of your revision by ticking off each topic heading in the book. You may find it helpful to add your own notes as you work through each topic.

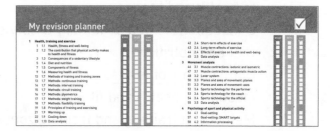

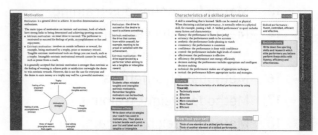

Features to help you succeed

Exam tips

Expert tips are given throughout the book to help you polish your exam technique in order to maximise your chances in the exam.

Typical mistakes

The author identifies the typical mistakes candidates make and explains how you can avoid them.

Now test yourself

These short, knowledge-based questions provide the first step in testing your learning. Answers are at the back of the book.

Definitions and key words

Clear, concise definitions of essential key terms are provided where they first appear.

Key words from the specification are highlighted in bold throughout the book.

Revision activities

These activities will help you to understand each topic in an interactive way.

Exam practice

Practice exam questions are provided for each topic. Use them to consolidate your revision and practise your exam skills.

Online

Go online to check your answers to the exam questions at **www.hoddereducation.co.uk/myrevisionnotes**

Data Analysis

These examples will help you to practise your Data Analysis skills in the context of each chapter's content. Answers are online at **www.hoddereducation.co.uk/myrevisionnotes**

My revision planner

	REVISED	TESTED	EXAM READY

Countdown to my exams

2–6 weeks to go

- Read through the relevant sections of this book and refer to the exam tips, exam summaries, typical mistakes and key terms. Tick off the topics as you feel confident about them. Highlight those topics you find difficult and look at them again in detail.
- Test your understanding of each topic by working through the 'Now test yourself' questions in the book. Look up the answers at the back of the book.
- Make a note of any problem areas as you revise, and ask your teacher to go over these in class.
- Look at past papers. They are one of the best ways to revise and practise your exam skills. Write or prepare planned answers to the exam practice questions provided in this book. Check your answers online at **www.therevisionbutton.co.uk/myrevisionnotes**
- Use the revision activities to try out different revision methods. For example, you can make notes using mind maps, spider diagrams or flash cards.
- Track your progress using the revision planner and give yourself a reward when you have achieved your target.

REVISED ☐

One week to go

- Try to fit in at least one more timed practice of an entire past paper and seek feedback from your teacher, comparing your work closely with the mark scheme.
- Check the revision planner to make sure you haven't missed out any topics. Brush up on any areas of difficulty by talking them over with a friend or getting help from your teacher.
- Attend any revision classes put on by your teacher. Remember, he or she is an expert at preparing people for exams.

REVISED ☐

The day before the exam

- Flick through these Revision Notes for useful reminders, for example, the exam tips, how to prepare for the exam, typical mistakes and key terms.
- Check the time and place of your exam.
- Make sure you have everything you need — extra pens and pencils, tissues, a watch, bottled water, sweets.
- Allow some time to relax and have an early night to ensure you are fresh and alert for the exam.

REVISED ☐

Introduction

There is no single tried and tested way to revise that works for everyone. You must find your own method but remember to replicate examination conditions in that:

- you cannot bring notes in
- you are under time pressure.

Mind maps or **spider diagrams** can be a great way to build up your ability to recall information without having the benefit of your notes. Simply choose a specific topic area and, without your notes, write down what you can remember. When you feel you cannot remember any further information, consult your notes then start again.

Sample examination questions are one of the most important revision tools you have. The examination board produces sample assessment materials and mark schemes, which can be of great benefit to you to test yourself on the types of questions that could appear in the paper.

Revision cards are a great way to rewrite your notes in a small, concise but manageable format. Create topic cards with the main points to remember or create questions on one side with the answers on the other.

Study buddies can be great in that you can ask each other questions and learn from each other. It is often a good idea if you both try past examination questions and then compare each other's answers. You can download old WJEC/Eduqas questions from their website.

As a definitive plan for the examination, it may be an idea to adopt the principle of Time, Topic, Command, Context (TTCC). In simple terms this involves going through four stages to answer every question in the examination:

1 Time: Look at the number of marks and multiply this by one, then take a small amount of time off. For example a 4–mark question would give you approximately 3 minutes.
2 Topic: Once you know how long you have got, read the question to work out what the topic area being examined is. This may involve reading the question several times.
3 Command: Check that you have seen and highlighted or underlined the main command word/s within the question so that you know what the examiner expects; for example, if you see Explain, it means you need to give detail and set out reasons.
4 Context: Read the question again (and again if necessary) to work out the context; that means, what is it actually asking me to do?

If you were looking at the following question, the four stages of TTCC can be applied.

1 State what happens to tidal volume and inspiratory reserve volume as a result of starting to exercise. [2 marks]
- **T** – 2 marks = take just less than 2 minutes
- **T** – The topic is tidal volume and inspiratory reserve volume (lung volumes)
- **C** – The command word is state
- **C** – The context is to state, therefore stating that tidal volume increases and inspiratory reserve volume decreases

It is also important never to leave questions out altogether. You may pick up marks even with an educated guess! Good luck!

The WJEC and Eduqas Specifications for GCSE PE are generally the same as one another. The minor differences between the two specifications have been highlighted in Table 0.1 to indicate where they are included in the revision guide.

Table 0.1 The differences between the specifications

WJEC specification	Eduqas specification	Where the italicised content is covered
The functions of nutrients … .	The functions of nutrients. *The role of nutrients in different intensities of exercise to include carbohydrates, proteins, fats, vitamins and hydration. The dangers of under and over hydrating … .*	Diet and nutrition Page 5
Different methods of training including continuous, interval (including fartlek), circuit, weight training and plyometrics.	Different methods of training including continuous, interval, including fartlek, circuit, weight training and plyometrics. *Flexibility training including active, passive, dynamic stretching.*	Methods of training and training zones Page 13
Training zones and the link to heart rate, exercise, fitness, energy systems and health.	Training zones and the link to heart rate, exercise, fitness, energy systems and health. *Aerobic training zone to develop cardiovascular system. Anaerobic training zone to develop lactic acid system. Calculation of maximum heart rate and percentages for different training zones.*	Methods of training and training zones Page 13
The structure of the skeletal system to include ball and socket, hinge and pivot joints (synovial joints); major bones including radius, ulna, humerus, femur, tibia, fibula.	The structure of the skeletal system to include ball and socket, hinge and pivot joints (synovial joints); major bones including radius, ulna, humerus, femur, tibia, fibula. *Flat bones such as scapula, cranium and ribs for protection.*	Muscular-skeletal system Page 25
The structure of the muscular system. Links of major muscles to types of movement at different joints including flexion, extension, adduction, abduction, circumduction, rotation.	The structure of the muscular system. Links of major muscles to types of movement at different joints including flexion, extension, adduction, abduction, circumduction, rotation. *Links of major muscles to types of muscle contractions (concentric, eccentric and isometric).*	Muscular-skeletal system Page 29
Functions to include gaseous exchange, *diffusion, haemoglobin,* oxygenation of blood.	Functions to include gaseous exchange, oxygenation of blood.	Cardio-respiratory and vascular systems Page 31
The characteristics and factors affecting aerobic/anaerobic exercise including intensity, duration, *nutrients, waste products, nutrients for fuel and recovery.* *The role of nutrients in different intensities of exercise to include carbohydrates, proteins, fats and hydration. The dangers of under and overhydrating.*	The characteristics and factors affecting aerobic/anaerobic exercise including intensity and duration.	Aerobic and anaerobic exercise Page 39
Personal experiences that impact upon participation.	*Up to date strategies* and personal experiences that impact upon participation.	Participation Page 68
Reformative policies such as anti-racism campaigns, e.g. Kick It Out, adapted sports for disabled people.	(Strategies not covered in this specification.)	Strategies to improve participation in sport and physical activity Page 75

Exam practice and Data analysis answers at **www.hoddereducation.co.uk/myrevisionnotes**

1 Health, training and exercise

Health, fitness and well-being

Health includes three different factors, which must all be present for a person to be deemed 'healthy': mental, physical and social (health and **well-being**). The absence of any of these components may well mean that the person is lacking in an aspect of health.

- **Mental health and well-being** relates to: coping with the normal stresses of life, working productively while being able to make a contribution to your community or place of residence.
- **Physical health and well-being** relates to: all of the body's systems are working well, so you are free from illness or infirmity. You therefore have the ability to carry out everyday tasks and complete your job/daily demands.
- **Social health and well-being** relates to: basic human needs being met (e.g. food, clothing and shelter) while suffering little stress in social circumstances. You have friendship and support and welcome the company of other people.

Fitness is key when performing everyday tasks. In some jobs, such as being in the army, a suitably high fitness level is required to perform the tasks safely and efficiently. Some jobs require a lower fitness level, such as when a person is sitting down at a desk in front of a computer all day.

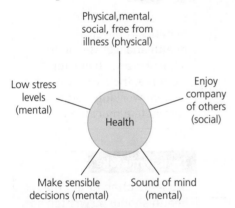

Figure 1.1 Health, fitness and well-being

> **Health**: (as per the World Health Organization's definition, 1948) 'A state of complete physical, mental and social well-being and not merely the absence of disease or infirmity.'
>
> **Well-being**: feeling content, comfortable and happy due to a mixture of physical, mental and social health factors.
>
> **Fitness**: meeting the demands of the environment, also known as physical readiness for an activity.

Exam tip

As well as knowing the definitions, it is important that you can identify and explain the contribution that physical activity makes to health and fitness. Remember that physical exercise enables the 'feel good' hormone *serotonin* to be released in the body!

Revision activity

On a blank piece of paper try to write down the definitions of:
- health
- fitness.

Exam practice

1 Identify the aspects that are part of health. Tick **one** box only. [1]
  a physical aspects ☐
  b mental aspects ☐
  c social aspects ☐
  d all of the above ☐
2 Describe the difference between fitness and well-being. [4]
3 Identify **four** aspects of health and well-being. [4]

ONLINE ☐

Now test yourself

1 What are the three components of health and well-being?
2 How does fitness relate to everyday life?

TESTED ☐

The contribution that physical activity makes to health and fitness

REVISED

Being physically active holds many benefits to health and fitness. The main benefits are summarised in Table 1.1.

Table 1.1 The benefits of being physically active

The benefits of being physically active	
Physical health and well-being	<ul><li>improved function of the body's major systems, e.g. cardiovascular system</li><li>increased efficiency of heart function</li><li>reduces chances of developing some diseases, e.g. diabetes</li><li>ability to carry out everyday tasks without getting tired</li></ul>
Mental health and well-being	<ul><li>reduces stress levels</li><li>releases 'feel-good' hormones in the body such as serotonin</li><li>enables a person to control their emotions and work productively in their day-to-day tasks</li><li>improves confidence</li></ul>
Social health and well-being	<ul><li>provides opportunities to socialise/make friends</li><li>encourages co-operation skills with others</li><li>encourages team-working skills</li><li>ensures that essential human needs are provided (clothing/shelter)</li></ul>
Fitness level	<ul><li>fitness levels increase with activity</li><li>body can cope easier with daily demands and potentially do more before fatigue sets in</li></ul>

Revision activity

On a blank piece of paper write down the following terms:
- Physical health and well-being
- Mental health and well-being
- Social health and well-being

Now try to write down an aspect associated with these terms.

Exam tip

Be prepared to link the benefits of physical health and well-being to a particular activity, for example, the cardiovascular system working well to complete a marathon.

The benefits of physical exercise can be seen in all aspects of health. Physical benefits help you to meet the demands of your daily life, improve your fitness, give you access to social opportunities and keep you feeling in a positive mental state.

Typical mistake

Students often forget that health should be written as health and well-being.

Now test yourself

TESTED

1 Name one benefit of physical health and well-being.
2 Name one benefit of mental health and well-being.
3 Name one benefit of social health and well-being.

Exam practice

1 Identify four benefits of being physically active. [4]
2 Describe and explain how a high level of fitness could help a person (other than an athlete) to perform their work in a physically demanding career. [2]
3 Describe the difference between social and mental health. [4]

ONLINE

Exam practice and Data analysis answers at **www.hoddereducation.co.uk/myrevisionnotes**

As human beings, we make choices every day as to how we live our lives. These choices can be informed – what we have been told we should do – or spontaneous and carefree – what we feel like doing at that specific point in time.

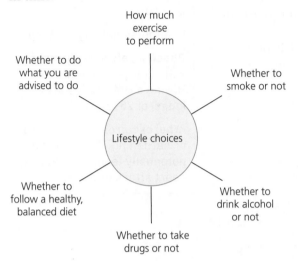

Figure 1.2 Lifestyle choices

Most people know that **lifestyle** choices should be healthy and some people are **motivated** to **adhere** to these suggestions. However, some people are not motivated to follow these guidelines. Why is this? Possible reasons are shown in Figure 1.3.

Figure 1.3 Reasons for making poor lifestyle choices

> **Lifestyle**: involves the choices we make about how we live our lives.
>
> **Adherence and motivation**: refers to conforming to suggested rules or suggestions, whilst having the internal drive to do so (or not).

Choosing to follow a **sedentary lifestyle** involves making a choice to have no or irregular physical activity. This can be very damaging for the health and well-being of an individual. As a result, the motivation to adhere to the 'norms' of being physically active and healthy may well reduce. Other consequences of a sedentary lifestyle include:

- increased levels of stress (mental health and well-being)
- possible development of **hypertension** (physical health and well-being)
- possible **insomnia** (physical health and well-being)
- possible development of **obesity** (physical health and well-being)
- possible development of **atherosclerosis** (physical health and well-being)
- potential poor self-esteem (mental health and well-being)
- development of a poor body image and self-confidence (mental health and well-being)
- having few friends (social health and well-being).

Sedentary lifestyle: refers to a person's lifestyle choice to have no or irregular physical activity.

Hypertension: high blood pressure.

Insomnia: inability to sleep.

Obesity: refers to a person with a large fat content. Having a BMI (body mass index) of 25 or over.

Atherosclerosis: narrowing or hardening of the arteries, potentially leading to angina, heart attack or stroke.

Revision activity

Martin is a teenage boy who gets a lift to school, eats fast food and takes part in a limited amount of physical activity

List what lifestyle choices Martin could make to potentially improve his health and well-being.

Exam tip

Remember the negative effect of a sedentary lifestyle using **SLOW**:
- **S**leep loss
- **L**evels of stress increased
- **O**besity – causing weight gain
- **W**on't have as many friends

Typical mistake

It is common for students to forget that a sedentary lifestyle choice can affect all three components of health (physical, mental and social).

The consequences of a sedentary lifestyle affect physical, mental and social health and well-being. It can prove to be a 'downward spiral' where less exercise leads to poor eating habits, weight gain and a feeling of tiredness and lethargy. This may lead to depression and being unwilling to conform to living a healthy, active lifestyle.

You should refer to Chapter 5 for strategies to improve participation in sport and physical activity.

Now test yourself

TESTED

1 What is a sedentary lifestyle?
2 Think of one reason why a sedentary lifestyle is chosen.

Exam practice

1 Identify **four** factors that may cause an individual to lack the motivation to adhere to suggested lifestyle choices. [4]
2 In 2015, nearly four million people in Britain died from disease related to their weight. Evaluate how choosing a sedentary lifestyle could affect your weight and subsequently your health. [6]

ONLINE

Diet and nutrition

Human beings should consume an appropriate amount of calories to satisfy their energy demands. The amount consumed can result in the following outcomes:

- **Energy is balanced**: this means that the amount consumed equals the amount needed and no weight is put on or lost.
- **Positive energy balance**: this means that the amount consumed is greater than what was needed, resulting in weight gain.
- **Negative energy balance**: this means that the amount consumed is less than what was needed, resulting in weight loss.

Calorie intake should come from a **balanced diet** of carbohydrates, fats, protein, minerals and water. To have a truly 'balanced diet' the body should consume approximately:

- 55–60 per cent carbohydrate
- 25–30 per cent fat
- 15–20 per cent protein.

The required calorie intake depends upon what the person is doing that day. For example, a manual job will require more energy whereas a sedentary office job requires less.

> **Energy balance**: the relationship between intake of food and output of work, so calories consumed to those used. The energy balance is positive when the body stores extra food as fats (more consumed than needed) and negative when the body draws on stored fat to provide energy (more needed than consumed).
>
> **Balanced diet**: eating the right amount of calories from varying sources to deal with the energy that will be needed.

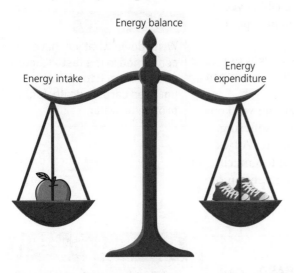

Figure 1.4 The energy balance refers to the balance of what you consume (calories) to what you use

> **Exam tip**
>
> You should take particular notice of the link between nutrient use and the intensity of exercise.

A breakdown of what each nutrient contributes within the body is shown in Table 1.2. The table also shows suitable food sources of each nutrient.

Table 1.2 Nutrients and what they are needed for

Nutrient	Specific need
Carbohydrate	<ul><li>The main and preferred energy source for all types of activity.</li><li>Required for high and low intensity energy.</li><li>Works as a fuel for muscular contractions, acting as the main fuel for medium to high intensity exercise (80% or higher anaerobic activity).</li><li>Particularly useful for 1 min to 2 hours of exercise.</li><li>Provided within bread, pasta, potatoes and starch-based foodstuffs.</li></ul>
Fats	<ul><li>Also an energy source.</li><li>Required for low intensity energy and insulation. Low intensity is aerobic (60% or lower of maximal heart rate)</li></ul>

Nutrient	Specific need

	● Comes in two forms:
	  ● saturated fat (usually animal fat)
	  ● unsaturated fat (vegetable fat/oils)
	● NB: saturated fat can be responsible for clogging arteries.

Protein	● Required for tissue growth and repair. ● It has a small part to play in energy. ● Provided by foodstuffs like fish, meat, eggs, dairy products and nuts.
Minerals	● Required for bone growth and the maintenance of regular body functions. ● Inorganic substances, e.g. calcium, are good for bone formation.
Water	● Required to prevent dehydration. ● Approximately eight 8-ounce glasses should be drunk in an average day.

Typical mistake

Students often forget the difference between the use of carbohydrates and fat, simply stating they are both for energy. Remember fat is used at a low intensity, whereas carbohydrates tend to be used at all intensities (but hold particular relevance for medium to high intensity).

Suitable nutrition and a balanced diet of varying nutrients enable overall health to be maintained and can hold varying roles in different types of physical activity. For example:
- **Carbohydrate** is consumed in large quantities before the event by endurance athletes (called carbohydrate loading) so that it does not run out during the event.
- **Protein** is consumed to assist in muscle repair after a training workout.
- **Water** maintains hydration, preventing reaction time from suffering, decision-making from slowing, heart rate from increasing etc. A lack of water can affect the judgement of distances and objects; too much water can be dangerous. Hyponatremia results from over-retention of water in the body and is where the water enters the tissue cells rather than staying in the blood.

Revision activity

Write down what you have consumed in the last 24 hours and label each foodstuff or liquid as carbohydrate, fat, protein or water.

Exam tip

Remember the effects of dehydration by using the word **HARD**:
- **H**eart rate **A**ccelerates
- **R**eaction time increases (gets slower)
- **D**ecision-making slows.

Now test yourself

1 What is carbohydrate for?
2 What is fat for?
3 What is protein for?

TESTED

Exam practice

1 Identify the type of activity for which carbohydrates are a particularly important source of energy. Tick **one** box only. [1]
  a low intensity ☐
  b low to medium intensity activities ☐
  c medium intensity activities ☐
  d medium to high intensity activities ☐
2 Name and describe three negative effects of not drinking enough water. (WJEC only) [3]
3 Explain why it is important to include fats and protein in a balanced diet. (Eduqas only) [2]

ONLINE

Components of fitness

The components of fitness are shown in Table 1.3 with their relevant definition.

Table 1.3 **Components of fitness**

Component	Definition
Cardiovascular endurance	The ability of the heart and lungs to supply oxygen to the working muscles.
Muscular endurance	The ability of a muscle or muscle group to undergo repeated contractions avoiding fatigue.
Muscular strength	The ability to overcome a resistance.
Flexibility	The range of movement possible at a joint.
Body composition	Body type/shape; also known as somatotype: ectomorph, mesomorph and endomorph.
Agility	The ability to move and change direction quickly (at speed) while maintaining control.
Speed	The maximum rate at which an individual is able to perform a movement or cover a distance in a period of time. It is also defined as putting the body parts into action as quickly as possible.
Power	Explosive strength or anaerobic power is the product of strength and speed, i.e. strength × speed.
Co-ordination	The ability to use different (two or more) parts of the body together smoothly and efficiently.
Balance	The maintenance of the centre of mass over the base of support.
Reaction time	The time taken to initiate a response to a stimulus.

Figure 1.5 Balance being used in a static position

> **Exam tip**
>
> It is important that you know what each component of fitness is and when it is needed in sport.

Table 1.4 shows the components of fitness, examples of when these components are needed, and an example of how developed fitness levels can affect lifestyle.

Table 1.4 Components of fitness and how they are used

Component	Sporting example	Lifestyle/ performance application
Cardiovascular endurance	Supplying oxygen to the muscles for the duration of a marathon	Being able to walk throughout the day without getting tired
Muscular endurance	Continual rowing action in a 200m race	Repeatedly using leg muscles to walk throughout the day
Muscular strength	Throwing a punch in boxing	Lifting equipment/heavy items
Flexibility	Performing splits in gymnastics	Bending down to pick something up
Body composition	Rugby players are often mesomorph with broad shoulders and large muscle content	Muscular frame to perform manual labour tasks
Agility	Changing direction on a tennis court to retrieve an opponent's shot	Changing direction to prevent a collision when walking
Speed	100m race	Running to catch a bus
Power	Quickly pushing out of the blocks in a 200m sprint	Hammering a nail
Co-ordination	Co-ordinating arms and legs to perform a running action	Catching a ball
Balance	Static balance is needed for a held move, e.g. handstand, whereas dynamic balance is needed when moving, e.g. running	Standing on toes to reach for an object
Reaction time	Reaction to an opponent's shot in table tennis before the ball hits the floor	Playing computer games

Typical mistake

Students regularly state what components of fitness are needed for an activity but fail to fully justify why. For example:
● Tennis players need agility to change direction at speed. (not fully justified)
● Tennis players need agility to change direction at speed as if they are moving one way, and the ball is hit the other way, they will need to change direction quickly enough to get to the ball before it bounces out. (fully justified)

Now test yourself

TESTED

1 What is agility?
2 What is cardiovascular endurance?
3 When would you need speed in sport?

Exam practice

1 What is agility, and why is agility needed to play tennis? (Eduqas only) [2]
2 Describe one method of training that could be used to develop agility. (Eduqas only) [2]
3 What is cardiovascular endurance and why is it required to run a marathon? (Eduqas only) [2]
4 Evaluate, using examples, the importance of agility and reaction time to a 100m runner. [6]

ONLINE

Figure 1.6 Long-distance runners require cardiovascular endurance to supply oxygen to the working muscles for long periods of time

Revision activity

Using your favourite sport, choose which components of fitness are needed in that sport. Justify your choices.

Carrying out a variety of fitness tests can be useful in many ways. The main advantages to be gained are:

- identifying strengths and weaknesses, such as which fitness components require some specific training to improve them
- identifying a baseline level of fitness that can then be improved
- comparison of previous to current levels of fitness
- monitoring improvement, for example, has training improved specific fitness levels
- it can be used as a motivational tool, providing variety to training sessions.

In learning about fitness tests, a basic set of rules operates:

- What is the name of the test?
- How do you carry out the test to ensure validity?
- What component/s of fitness does the test actually measure?

Exam tip

You can remember some of the reasons for fitness testing by using the word **SWIM**:
- (Identify) **S**trengths
- (Identify) **W**eaknesses
- (Monitor) **I**mprovement
- **M**otivation (used to motivate performers)

Table 1.5 Table of fitness tests

Fitness test	Protocol	Component of fitness
Multi-stage fitness test	<ul><li>Individual runs 20m in time with bleeps</li><li>The time between bleeps gets shorter as the level increases</li><li>The individual keeps running until they cannot keep up with the bleeps</li><li>The score is recorded as a level and bleep, e.g. level 8 bleep 4, and compared to national averages.</li></ul>	Cardiovascular endurance
Cooper's 12-minute run test	<ul><li>Flat surface or oval track is used</li><li>Distance covered in 12 minutes is recorded</li><li>Compared to national averages</li></ul>	Cardiovascular endurance
Abdominal curl test	<ul><li>Lie on the mat in sit-up position, partner supports ankles</li><li>Sit up on the bleep and down on the bleep (staying in time)</li><li>It is a progressive test – the bleeps get faster</li><li>Record score: how many sit-ups you complete</li><li>Scores are compared to national averages</li></ul>	Muscular endurance
Press-up test	<ul><li>Many different methods of performing this test</li><li>One method involves adopting a 'modified' press-up position with the legs higher than the hands</li><li>Count how many press-ups can be done in 60 seconds or until exhaustion</li></ul>	Muscular endurance
Hand grip test	<ul><li>Dynamometer should be held in the individual's dominant hand</li><li>Squeeze with maximum effort and record score</li><li>Repeat three times and record best score</li><li>Compare to national averages</li></ul>	Strength
1-rep max test	<ul><li>Lift a weight once using the correct technique</li><li>If completed, attempt a heavier weight until the heaviest weight the individual can possibly lift once is discovered</li><li>If a weight cannot be lifted, a lighter weight should be used to calculate the maximum weight that can be lifted</li></ul>	Strength
Sit and reach test	<ul><li>Adopt a sitting position on the floor with legs straight</li><li>Shoes should be removed and feet should be flat against the sit and reach board</li><li>Slider (if available) should be set to 14cm to be in line with the toes</li><li>The individual reaches forward and pushes the slider as far as possible</li><li>Score is recorded in cm and compared to national averages</li></ul>	Flexibility

➜

Fitness test	Protocol	Component of fitness
Skin fold calliper test	• Several areas/ sites of the body are used • Skinfolds are grasped between thumb and index finger and lifted 1 cm (pinch and pull) • The callipers are used to measure the size of the skinfold at each site	Body composition
Illinois agility test	• Performer starts face down on the floor • The test involves running round the cones (10m × 5m) • As fast as possible (it is a maximal test) • It is timed in seconds, and • Can be compared to national averages	Agility
30/50m sprint	• Using a 'flying/moving' start • The individual is timed running 30/50m as fast as they can • The score in seconds is compared to national averages	Speed
Vertical jump test	• Feet flat, stand and push the wall ruler with the fingertips as high as possible • This provides the individual's 'zero point' • Apply chalk (or something to make a mark) to the fingertips • From a standing position, the individual jumps as high as possible, marking the ruler with the chalk • The observer records the height jumped in cm • The score is compared to national averages	(Leg) Power
Stork balance test	• Start balanced on two flat feet • Hands are placed on the hips • One leg is lifted so that the toes of the lifted leg touch the inside of the knee of the planted leg • Timekeeper tells the individual to raise the heel on the planted leg (and the stopwatch should start) • Balance on one leg for as long as possible until the loss of balance or toes attached to the inside of the knee are moved • Time is recorded in minutes/seconds • Scores are compared to national averages	Balance
Alternate hand throw test	• Tennis ball starts in one hand • Both feet together, 2m from the wall • When 'go' is called the time starts – 30 seconds' duration • The individual throws the ball against the wall and catches the ball with the opposite hand • Repeats as many times as possible • 2 attempts are allowed • The score is compared to national averages	Co-ordination
Ruler drop test	• One person holds a metre ruler at the zero point (vertically) • Person being tested places their thumb and index finger of their dominant hand around the ruler (but not touching it) at 50cm • Without warning the ruler is released • The individual being tested must react to the drop and catch the ruler as fast as they can (with their thumb and index finger) • Score is recorded in cm; how far from 50cm does the individual catch the ruler • 3 attempts are allowed	Reaction time

Revision activity

Choose a team sport. Identify the main components of fitness that are needed for that sport and revise how these components could be suitably tested.

Typical mistake

Students often write that the multi-stage fitness test is run over 25m when in fact it is run over 20m.

Now test yourself

1 Think of two reasons why fitness tests are done.
2 Name two fitness tests and describe what they test.

Exam practice

A PE teacher is in charge of a group of GCSE PE students. The teacher decides to assess their fitness before writing training programmes to improve their fitness for their respective sports.

1 Explain **two** possible reasons why it would be important to measure the students' initial fitness. (WJEC only)   [4]
2 Describe how the students' cardiovascular endurance could be tested. (WJEC only)   [2]
3 Explain why fitness is as important for a PE teacher as it is for their students.   [3]
4 Five of the students in the class do the following sports/activities:

Student	Main activity
1	100m sprinter
2	Cross-country runner
3	Gymnastics
4	Trampoline
5	Tennis

Complete the table below by identifying a suitable component of fitness for each student to develop, and naming a suitable test to test that component.   [5]

Student	Main activity	Component	Test
1	100m sprinter		
2	Cross-country runner		
3	Gymnastics		
4	Trampoline		
5	Tennis		

ONLINE

As well as the main fitness tests, there are other measurement tools including health questionnaires and screening methods such as monitoring blood pressure, heart rate, calorie input and expenditure.

- **Health questionnaires** are often used by employers to decide whether a potential employee is fit and healthy enough to perform the job. They can also form part of a doctor's initial assessment of a patient's health.
- **Screening methods** include the use of heart rate monitors and blood pressure readers to assess if the heart is beating healthily and to check that blood pressure is in the 'normal' range. (Normal ranges are included in the cardiac values section on page 34.) Any potential problems with the heart can be detected early to prevent further problems. If blood pressure is too high or low, it can be a sign of a medical condition, which may require the administering of drugs or surgery/intervention.
- **Calorie input and output** Hand-held sensors can be used to detect the calorific value of foods. However, detecting the intake of calories compared to the output allows performers to maintain, lose or put on weight accordingly.

> **Protocol**: how the test is carried out. Tests should be carried out correctly to increase the chances of validity.
>
> **Validity**: means that a test will test what it states it tests, i.e. the Illinois agility test should actually test agility.
>
> **Reliability**: tests are reliable if they are repeated and can give similar results.

Measuring health and fitness can help to plan training programmes, assess strengths and weaknesses, etc.

↓

Tests performed should follow the stated protocol

↓

Following the protocol increases the chances of validity

↓

If tests can be repeated and provide similar results, this increases the chances of the tests being reliable

Figure 1.7 Measuring health and fitness

Exam tip

Remember the concept of reliability by remembering the three **RE**s:
- **RE**liability involves
- **RE**peating tests and gaining similar
- **RE**sults

Exam practice

1 What is agility, and why is agility needed to play tennis? (Eduqas only) [2]
2 The multi-stage fitness test is an appropriate fitness test that netball players could use to monitor their level of fitness. Explain one reason why this is an appropriate test for a netball player. (WJEC only) [4]
3 The vertical jump test is an appropriate test that netball players could use to monitor their level of fitness. Explain one reason why this is an appropriate test for a netball player. (WJEC only) [4]

ONLINE

Now test yourself

1 What is reliability?
2 What is validity?
3 What does protocol mean?

TESTED

Methods of training and training zones

Different methods of training should be used depending on the specific needs of a performer. These needs can include:

- demands of the sport being played, e.g. position
- current fitness levels
- intended fitness levels
- age, health, motivation, etc.

Methods: continuous training

Continuous training involves any exercise that can be maintained without rest and repeated over and over, for example, running, rowing and swimming. Continuous training is used to improve cardiovascular endurance and involves working at a constant rate or intensity. This is often referred to as 'steady state exercise'. Any sport that requires the need to 'keep going' for a long period of time can benefit from continuous training, for example, marathon running, football (90 minutes), rugby (80 minutes) etc. However, athletes performing long-distance running where the intensity remains relatively stable can benefit the most.

Figure 1.8 Running is a typical continuous training activity

Energy system and intensity

Continuous training is intended to work the aerobic energy system. To do this, it is most common to use your heart rate as a guide. This is known as working at your 'aerobic training zone'. Maintaining aerobic activity will reduce fat content, and suitably stress the heart so that it gets stronger and potentially larger and more efficient. Performers may be able to work steadily for longer in their games or events. Continuous training usually involves working without rests, for approximately 20 minutes or more.

Calculating the aerobic training zone for continuous training involves using your heart rate as a guide. This involves calculating your maximum heart rate in beats per minute and working at a percentage of this:

- calculate maximum heart rate (220 minus age)
- calculate aerobic training zone (60–80 per cent of maximal heart rate).

> **Continuous training:** exercising for a sustained period of time without rest at steady state intensity.

> **Exam tip**
>
> To remember the calculation of intensity for continuous training (220 – age) you can use the saying '220 … is plenty'.

> **Typical mistake**
>
> Although continuous training is appropriate to team games, try to remember that the varying intensity of interval/fartlek training may be more beneficial as it matches the changing intensity required to play team sports.

Methods: interval training

Interval training is any type of training that involves alternating periods of work with periods of rest. It usually involves periods of intense exercise (working hard) with periods of rest or low intensity exercise. However, the work periods can be altered in length and intensity to mimic the sport being trained for.

Fartlek training

Fartlek training (or speed play) involves changing the intervals of work so that intensity and terrain vary, for example, walk, jog, sprint, jog (hill), walk and so on. This can result in improved cardiovascular fitness and anaerobic fitness. This training type mixes continuous training with interval training.

Energy systems and intensities for interval training

As interval training can be altered to suit the needs of a performer, the energy system being stressed can vary. High intensity interval training (HIIT) involves short, high intensity periods of work, which improves the anaerobic system.

You can also vary the length of the intervals in order to gain different benefits. For example:

- High intensity anaerobic intervals can last anywhere from 10 to 60 seconds.
- Low intensity and more aerobic intervals can last several minutes.
- Interval training can be altered to stress the aerobic and anaerobic energy systems.

Interval training: training method that incorporates periods of work interspersed with periods of rest.

Fartlek training: Swedish name for 'speed play' whereby the work rate intensity and terrain change from high to lower and back to higher.

Revision activity

Try to think of five sporting activities that would better suit the changing intensity of interval training compared to continuous training.

Now test yourself

1 What is continuous training?
2 What is interval training?
3 What is fartlek training?

TESTED

Exam practice

1 Which of the following activities would be better suited to interval or continuous training? Justify your answer. [6]

Sport	Interval or continuous training	Justification
Long-distance open water swimming		
Hockey		
Basketball		

2 A PE teacher is in charge of a group of GCSE PE students. After assessing their fitness, the teacher helps the students to write training programmes to improve their fitness for their respective sports.

One of the athletes competes in the 10,000m. Identify and explain a type of training that would help to develop the skills needed for this event. [3]

ONLINE

Methods: circuit training

Circuit training involves exercises being organised in different areas or stations. Each station can be completely different from the next. Completion of all of the stations is called 'a circuit'. The amount of rest between each station or after each circuit can be changed as necessary.

It is common that a circuit is designed to train different components of fitness and work on different muscles/body parts. Examples of common circuit training exercises include shuttle runs, step-ups, sit-ups, squat jumps, burpees, and so on.

> **Circuit training**: a series of exercises performed one after the other to complete 'a circuit' with a rest in between each circuit.

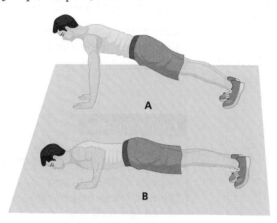

Figure 1.9 Push-ups can form part of a circuit training routine

Energy demand and intensity

The intensity of the work periods at stations can be changed. High intensity work rate will use the anaerobic system, whereas low intensity work can use the aerobic system. Performers should make sure the stations involve muscles/movements and energy demands that are suitable for their sport.

> **Exam tip**
>
> If you are asked to evaluate the use of circuit training, remember it can be changed to suit the activity. Thus, altering the work:rest ratio within a circuit will determine what the fitness aim of the circuit is. So, you could allow less rest in a circuit when training for sporting activities that allow few rests.

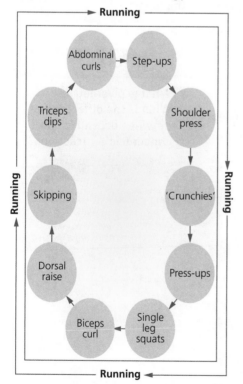

Figure 1.10 An example circuit, which includes running around the outside of the circuit and performing exercises at various stations

Methods: circuit training

Methods: plyometrics

Plyometrics is a type of training that is used to increase power (strength × speed). It usually involves bounding, hopping or jumping but can include medicine ball work, 'jump and clap' press-ups and box work (jumping on and off a box).

When bounding or depth jumping, an eccentric contraction causes a stronger concentric contraction. For example:
1 Quadriceps lengthen when landing (**eccentric contraction**).
2 'Elastic energy' is stored ready to be released through the next jump.
3 The second jump (using the stored elastic energy) makes use of a stronger **concentric contraction**.

The improvement in power is particularly useful for performers who need to use leg power to jump, for example, basketball players, triple jumpers, and so on.

Figure 1.11 The athlete is performing plyometrics by jumping onto and off the boxes. This is called box jumping

Plyometric work to improve power can put strain on joints, so correct technique should be used at all times.

Energy demand and intensity

Any athlete who requires power can use plyometrics and thus it tends to help the anaerobic elements of performance. A basketball player or a triple jumper may well use plyometrics to increase their leg power for jumping. The plyometric work is high intensity so usually involves rest periods in between exercises.

Plyometrics: power training that makes use of body weight involving an eccentric contraction, which results in a larger concentric contraction.

Eccentric contraction: lengthening of the muscle.

Concentric contraction: shortening of the muscle.

Typical mistake

It is common for students to suggest that plyometrics improves strength only. It improves strength *and* speed (power).

Revision activity

Design a circuit for a sport of your choice. Think about exercises that could be used to mimic the demands of that sport.

Now test yourself

1 What is plyometrics?
2 What is the difference between eccentric and concentric contractions?

TESTED

Exam practice

1 Identify the type of physical fitness that plyometric training is mostly used to improve. Tick **one** box only. [1]
   a aerobic fitness ☐
   b balance ☐
   c power ☐
   d reaction time ☐
2 Describe what is meant by the term work:rest ratio and explain why an understanding of work:rest ratio is important to athletes. (Eduqas only) [5]
3 Evaluate how relevant it would be for a basketball player to train using plyometrics. [3]

ONLINE

Exam practice and Data analysis answers at **www.hoddereducation.co.uk/myrevisionnotes**

Methods: weight training

Weight training involves using some resistance to develop muscular strength or muscular endurance. The weight being lifted may well be a free weight or a resistance machine. The lifting of weights tends to involve sets and reps where:

- a **repetition (rep)** is one complete lift of the weight
- a **set** is a group of several repetitions.

In all types of weight training, it is vital that the correct technique is adopted. Particular care should be taken with the performer's back as they should maintain a straight back as much as possible. Weight training may also involve a 'spotter' to spot for any difficulty when lifting a heavy weight.

Energy demand and intensity

The intensity of the weight being lifted should be chosen to meet the intended outcome. Thus heavy weights tend to be for muscular strength whereas lighter weights tend to be for muscular endurance. To calculate the intensity, the concept of a **1-rep max** is used. This is the maximum weight that can safely be lifted in one repetition. As a basic rule the following guidelines can be used:

- Muscular strength training: approximately 80 per cent or more of 1-rep max (3–5 sets of 2–6 repetitions).
- Muscular endurance: approximately 50–60 per cent of 1-rep max (3 sets of 12–15 repetitions).

Improvements in strength as a result of weight training can aid sports performance, for example, the strength used in a rugby tackle could improve. Equally, improvements in muscular endurance may help an athlete, for example, to maintain a race pace in a 1500m event. Weight training can improve body shape and body image, potentially improving self-esteem (mental health and well-being).

> **Repetition (rep)**: one complete lift of the weight.
>
> **Set**: a group of several repetitions.
>
> **1-rep max**: the maximum weight that can safely be lifted in one repetition.

> **Exam tip**
>
> If you are asked to evaluate the importance of weight training, try to link the improvement in muscular strength or endurance to the demands of the sport. For example, weight training is appropriate to a badminton player as improvements in strength may mean they can smash the shuttlecock with more force, making it harder to return.

Figure 1.12 Weight training can be used to improve muscular strength (heavy weights) or muscular endurance (light weights)

> **Now test yourself**
>
> 1 What is a repetition?
> 2 What is a set?
> 3 What is meant by '1-rep max'?
>
> TESTED

Exam practice

1 Identify which type of fitness heavy weights tend to be used to improve. Tick **one** box only. [1]
   a cardiovascular endurance ☐
   b balance ☐
   c muscular endurance ☐
   d muscular strength ☐
2 Identify and explain a type of training that would help develop the fitness needed to perform a 100m sprint. [3]
3 Identify and explain a type of training that would help develop the fitness needed to perform a javelin throw. [3]
4 A student is a rugby player who wants to increase their strength. Identify and explain a type of training that would help to develop strength. [3]

ONLINE

Methods: flexibility training

REVISED

A performer may want to improve their flexibility to enhance their performance levels. This involves increasing the range of movement at a joint. There are various ways that flexibility training can be carried out:
- static stretching
- active stretching
- passive stretching
- dynamic stretching.

Static stretching

Static stretches involve stretching as far as possible and holding the stretch in position for up to 30 seconds. This is the most common type of stretching and can increase the range of movement at a joint. The position of the stretch is often held using resistance from the floor, a wall or a partner. Examples include simple calf (gastrocnemius) stretches and hamstring stretches.

Active stretching

Active stretching involves holding a stretch in place using the strength of your agonist muscle only. An example would be holding your leg in a high position with no help from a partner or other aid. The agonist muscles hold the stretch in place. It can be quite difficult to hold such active stretches. They are often used in activities like yoga and Pilates.

Passive stretching

Passive stretching is where you hold a stretch in place with the assistance of another body part or a partner. An example is an arm crossing across your chest being held at the wrist by the other hand. Many partner-assisted stretches involve a partner providing resistance, for example, lying on your back while your partner holds your ankle and stretches your hamstrings.

Dynamic stretches

Dynamic stretches make use of movement, which can be exaggerated to replicate some of the movements that are produced in the physical activity. Examples include heel flicks, lunges and arm circles. Stretches are not held as such; the movement goes through the range of movement but continues to move. These are often used once the body is warmed up or as part of a cool down.

Exam tip

The types of stretches and their explanation can be remembered with the acronym **DAPS**:
- **D**ynamic – **D**o the movement from the sport
- **A**ctive – **A**gonist muscle holds the stretch
- **P**assive – **P**artner assisted
- **S**tatic – **S**till/stationary held

Typical mistake

It is a common mistake for students to suggest that stretches should form the first part of a warm-up. Stretches should follow a pulse training activity.

Revision activity

As part of your revision, try to perform some active, passive, static and dynamic stretches. Explain to a study partner what each stretch is and why it is that type of stretch.

Exam practice

1 Which characteristic below is typical of a dynamic stretch? [1]
   a stretch is held ☐
   b stretch involves the assistance of a partner ☐
   c stretch involves movements used in the activity ☐
   d stretch is held by the agonist muscle only ☐
2 Describe the main characteristics of a static stretch. (WJEC only) [3]
3 Explain how dynamic stretches may form part of a warm-up. (Eduqas only) [3]

ONLINE ☐

Now test yourself

1 What is a static stretch?
2 What is a dynamic stretch?
3 What is a passive stretch?
4 What is an active stretch?

TESTED ☐

Principles of training and exercising

When designing a training programme, it is generally accepted that the programme should include the 'principles of training'. The principles are known as:

- **Specificity**
- **Progression**
- **Overload** (frequency, intensity, duration)
- **Variance**.

Specificity, progression, overload, variance: the principles of training.

Exam tip

You can remember the principles of training by remembering **SPOV**:
- **S**pecificity
- **P**rogression
- **O**verload (frequency, intensity, duration)
- **V**ariance.

You also need to remember that the principle of overload has three parts, which can be remembered by **FID**:
- **F**requency
- **I**ntensity
- **D**uration

You must be able to explain what the principles of training mean and how they can be applied:

- **Specificity** refers to training being specific to the movements, muscles used, and energy demands of the sport.
- **Progression** refers to making training harder when it becomes too easy so that the body can continue to adapt.
- **Overload** (frequency, intensity, duration) refers to suitably overloading the body more than normal so that adaptation occurs. This involves working at a suitable intensity, training frequently (but not over-training) and training for an appropriate length of time to cause appropriate adaptation.
- **Variance** refers to varying training to prevent boredom or a drop in motivation.

Typical mistake

Students often simply write that 'specificity' refers to training specifically. This is too simple and links should be made to specific movements, energy systems and use of muscles that are specific to the sport being trained for.

Revision activity

Write down the acronyms SPOV and FID and add what you can remember about the principles of training and overload.

Exam practice

1 Identify four principles of training. [4]
2 Identify the **three** aspects of overload that should govern a training programme. [3]
3 Explain how the idea of 'progression' is important within a training programme. (Eduqas only) [3]

ONLINE

Now test yourself

1 What are the principles of training?
2 What are the principles of overload?

TESTED

As part of your GCSE in Physical Education, one key skill is being able to apply the principles of training to propose a suitable training programme.

There are various steps to this process:
1 Identify strengths and weaknesses via fitness testing.
2 Prioritise areas to be improved that are appropriate to the sport or activity being trained for.
3 Devise a suitable programme of training applying the principles of training.
4 Re-test to monitor improvement.

Applying the principles of training to sedentary individuals

Jenny is overweight, unfit and leads a sedentary lifestyle. She does little to no exercise but wants to improve her general fitness and lose weight. Her aim is to complete a 5k run within six months.
- Training type: Continuous training
- Intensity: 60 per cent of heart rate max

Application of the principles of training:
- **S**pecificity: She will run/jog as this replicates the movements used in a 5k.
- **P**rogression: She will start running slowly for a short period of time and build this up (progress) when it gets too easy.
- **O**verload (intensity, frequency, duration): She will work at 60 per cent of heart rate max for 15 minutes, although she will aim to progress to 65 then 70 per cent for longer. She will train twice a week to start with and will hopefully progress to 3–4 times a week.
- **V**ariance: She will run different routes and mix treadmill work with some street running.

Key considerations: General health and well-being can be improved through exercising. A basic cardiovascular fitness level is needed before more specific components can be improved. In Jenny's case, continuous training can meet the demands of the principles of training to allow her to progress towards a 5k run.

Applying the principles of training to elite sportspeople

Mohammed is an elite level triple jumper. His coach has highlighted that he needs to improve his strength, as his speed is already an asset. He is hoping to compete in the Commonwealth Games in two years' time.
- Training type: Weight training
- Intensity: 4 sets of 6–8 repetitions at 75 per cent of 1-rep max.

Application of the principles of training:
- **S**pecificity: He will train the same muscles that he uses to jump.
- **P**rogression: He will start at 75 per cent of 1-rep max but will aim to reach 80 per cent when appropriate.
- **O**verload (frequency, intensity, duration): 4 sets of 6–8 repetitions at 75 per cent of 1-rep max during a 1-hour gym session twice a week.
- **V**ariance: He will use machines, kettle bells and free weights to prevent boredom.

Key considerations: At an elite level, training must be very specific to meet the demands of the sport. There will be a lot of leg muscle work (quadriceps, hamstrings and gastrocnemius) to meet the strength demands of running and jumping.

Exam tip

Students must be able to apply the principles of training to improve health for sedentary individuals and fitness for sports performers.

Typical mistake

It is a common error for students to always use 60–80 per cent of maximal heart rate as the intensity. Weight training, for example, requires a percentage of 1-rep max, not heart rate.

Now test yourself

1 Can you remember the correct intensity to improve strength?
2 Can you remember the correct intensity to improve cardiovascular endurance?
3 Should sedentary people aim to improve health or fitness as their first priority?

TESTED ☐

Exam practice

1 Why is cardiovascular endurance important to develop, above any other component of fitness, for the sedentary person? [2]
2 Identify and explain the type of training that would be most appropriate for a marathon runner. [3]
3 Identify three ways in which the principle of specificity can be applied to a training programme. [3]

ONLINE ☐

Warming up

Warming up is a vital component for a performer to ensure their body is ready for activity, without suffering injury or ill effects of exercise. Warming up consists of three major components:

1 Activity to raise heart rate
2 Stretching
3 Higher intensity and activity-specific movements

Any activity to raise heart rate must do so gradually. This may involve walking, jogging or a light swim, for example, as this will enable oxygen to get to the working muscles in a greater quantity.

Stretches should be completed safely and work on all major muscles that will be used during the sporting event being performed. Stretches performed may be static/active/passive/dynamic or proprioceptive neuromuscular facilitation (PNF).

Higher intensity work and activity-specific movements may consist of skill drills involving a ball (in ball games), performing specific movements or working on tactics and set plays.

Warming up has many benefits, both physiologically and psychologically. These benefits are summarised in Figure 1.13.

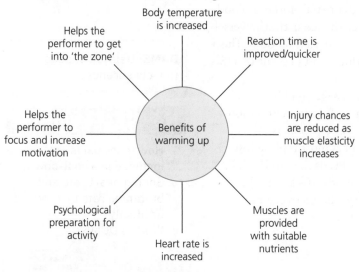

Figure 1.13 Benefits of warming up

> **Warming up:** gentle activity to prepare the body for exercise so that the chances of injury or ill effects are limited.

> **Exam tip**
>
> Remember that a warm-up has three components by using **ASH**:
> ● **A**ctivity to raise heart rate
> ● **S**tretching
> ● **H**igher intensity and activity-specific movements.

> **Revision activity**
>
> Try to design a warm-up that is suitable for a sport of your choice. The warm-up should include:
> 1 An activity to raise heart rate that is similar to the movement used in the sport.
> 2 Stretching – these can be static, active, passive, dynamic or PNF stretches but they must stretch the major muscles used in the sport.
> 3 Higher intensity and activity-specific movements that mimic the movements and skills used in the sport.

Exam practice

1 Identify the type of stretch that is partner-assisted. Tick **one** box only. [1]
   a dynamic stretch ☐
   b static stretch ☐
   c active stretch ☐
   d passive stretch ☐
2 Identify **three** physiological benefits of warming up. [3]

ONLINE ☐

Now test yourself

1 How many parts should a warm-up contain?
2 What should come first in a warm-up?
3 When should activity-specific movements take place?

TESTED ☐

Cooling down

As with warming up, cooling down is also a vitally important component of a sports performer's usual routine. Cooling down is often overlooked but its importance should not be ignored.

A cool-down could involve:

1 Activity to maintain elevated breathing and heart rate, for example, jogging. This activity should be gradually reduced in intensity.
2 Stretches, which should involve all major muscles that have been used.
3 A further recovery process, such as ice bath, massage, rehydration and nutrient intake.

Jogging is the most common activity to maintain then gradually reduce heart and breathing rate. However, such an activity can also be sport specific, for example, swimmers are likely to swim, rowers are likely to row, and so on.

Stretches must stretch the main muscles used. Stretches can be dynamic, active, passive, PNF or static, although static stretches are most commonly used in a cool-down (see page 18).

Further recovery processes can include:

● **Ice baths**: the performer enters the ice bath for a few minutes. The body's blood vessels vasoconstrict (reduce in diameter), forcing blood to the body's core. When the performer leaves the ice bath, the vessels vasodilate (increase in diameter), allowing oxygen-rich blood to flush the muscles. This helps to remove waste products and prevent **DOMS** – the delayed onset of muscle soreness.
● **Massage**: DOMS can also be prevented by massage. Rubbing and kneading of the muscles helps to reduce pain and assists with blood flow through the muscles, thus flushing out waste products.
● **Rehydration and nutrient intake**: performers must replace lost fluid to prevent dehydration, which can cause headaches and reduce decision-making and reaction time. Suitable foodstuffs should be consumed to replace lost nutrients/salts and aid the recovery process. This also prevents fainting or feelings of dizziness.

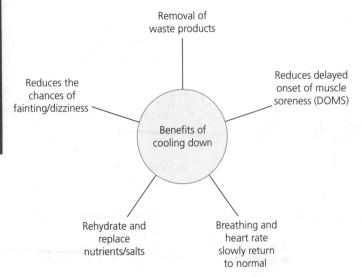

Figure 1.14 Benefits of cooling down

> **Typical mistake**
>
> Students often forget to include the need to rehydrate and replace nutrients/salts after cooling down.

> **Revision activity**
>
> Design a suitable cool-down for a sport of your choice.

> **DOMS**: Delayed onset of muscle soreness.

> ## Now test yourself
>
> 1 How many parts are included in a cool-down?
> 2 Should heart rate and breathing rate be reduced gradually?
> 3 What is DOMS?
>
> TESTED

> ## Exam practice
>
> 1 Describe what is meant by cooling down and explain why it is important to a performer. (Eduqas only) [5]
> 2 Identify **three** benefits of a suitable cool-down. [3]
> 3 Identify and explain **two** potential negative effects of not suitably cooling down. [4]
>
> ONLINE

Data analysis

Data demands of the specification require you to be able to interpret pie charts and tabled data sources, while interpreting and potentially presenting bar charts and line graphs.

Fitness testing example

A topic area like fitness testing could be a good source of data to interpret.

The tabled data below show the scores of a group of GCSE PE students who attempted the multi-stage fitness test.

Table 1.6 **The levels the students achieved**

Participant	Multi-stage fitness test score (level)
Boy 1	10
Boy 2	9
Boy 3	12
Boy 4	13
Boy 5	11
Girl 1	5
Girl 2	14
Girl 3	6
Girl 4	7
Girl 5	9

20 metres

Figure 1.15 **The multi-stage fitness test is run in 20m shuttles**

1 Analyse the tabled data to answer the following:
  a Who achieved the highest level? [1]
  b How many girls achieved level 6 or over? [1]
2 Analyse the data to present the scores for the boys in a bar chart. [6]
3 Suggest reasons why performers may have scored above level 10 in the multi-stage fitness test. [2]

Training regime example 1

This page requires you to analyse a pie chart to make conclusions. This is a key skill for your GCSE in Physical Education.

The pie chart in Figure 1.6 shows the weekly training habits of a small group of GCSE PE students, with some students:

● training once a week with continuous training
● weight training once a week
● training several times a week with mixed training types
● carrying out no training at all.

1 Analyse the pie chart. State what:
   a the most common training routine is for the group [1]
   b the least common training routine is for the group. [1]
2 Suggest reasons for the most common training routine. [4]

3 A percentage of the group does no training at all. Suggest possible consequences for this group of students of not taking part in any training. [4]

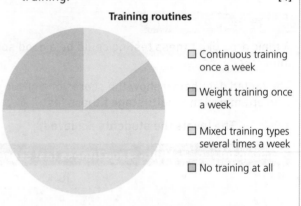

Training routines

☐ Continuous training once a week

☐ Weight training once a week

☐ Mixed training types several times a week

☐ No training at all

Figure 1.16 **Weekly training habits of some GCSE PE students**

Training regime example 2

Three friends have very different training regimes. They all train specifically for their sport and choose a suitable workload intensity to improve aspects of performance that are specific to their sport.

The tabled data below show the training types and intensities of three different performers.

Table 1.7 **Intensities of training**

Performer	Typical training intensity
1	● Running ● Steady state ● 60–80% of maximum heart rate for 30 minutes at a steady state
2	● Weight training ● 5 sets of 15 repetitions ● Working at 50% of 1-rep max
3	● Weight training ● 3 sets of 6 repetitions ● Working at 85% of 1-rep max

1 Analyse the information in the table.
   a What component of fitness is Performer 1 most likely to develop?
   b What component of fitness is Performer 2 most likely to develop?
   c What component of fitness is Performer 3 most likely to develop?
   d One of the performers is a long-distance runner. Which performer is this most likely to be. Justify your answer. [5]
2 Suggest two safety considerations that Performer 3 needs to consider when training. [2]
3 If Performer 1 decided to take up the sport of football, evaluate how appropriate their current training regime would be for that sport. [4]
4 Another friend joins the group. They are considering using fartlek training to improve their fitness for basketball. Evaluate how appropriate their choice of training type is. [3]

2 Exercise physiology

Structure of the skeletal system

The skeleton is made up of 206 bones. For GCSE PE, you need to know how muscles cause movement by pulling on the major bones.

The skeleton of the body provides many functions (see below). Bones meet at joints. There are several types of joint you need to know:

- synovial
- hinge
- ball and socket
- pivot.

Synovial joints

The internal structure of a synovial joint (Figure 2.2) includes many features that enable movement to occur freely and safely at the joint. Hinge, ball and socket and pivot joints are synovial joints. Synovial joints contain:

- a synovial membrane – to line the capsule of the joint
- synovial fluid – for lubrication
- cartilage pads at the end of bones – to absorb shock and ensure a friction-free, smooth surface
- ligaments – join bone to bone
- tendons – join bone to muscle
- bursae – fluid-filled bags that help to reduce friction.

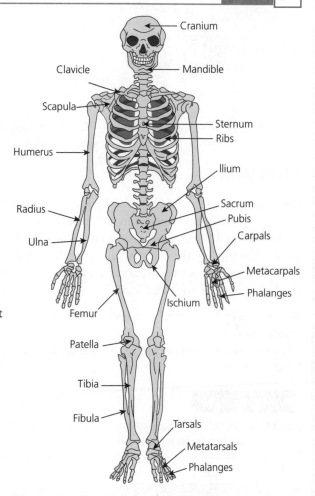

Figure 2.1 **The skeleton of the body**

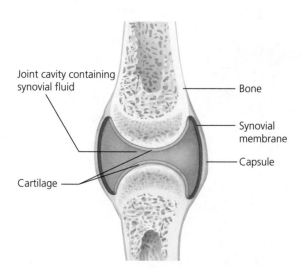

Figure 2.2 **The synovial joint**

Hinge joint

A hinge joint works like the hinge on a door. In Figure 2.3 the hinge joint at the elbow is shown, which allows bending of the arm (flexion) and straightening of the arm (extension). The knee and ankle are also hinge joints.

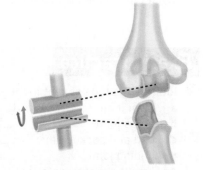

Figure 2.3 **The elbow joint is a hinge joint, moving just like the hinge on a door – forwards and backwards**

Ball and socket

A ball and socket joint provides a wide range of movement. The ball and socket at the shoulder (as shown in Figure 2.4) allows many movements to occur including flexion, extension, adduction, abduction, rotation and circumduction.

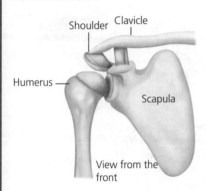

Figure 2.4 **The shoulder joint is a ball and socket joint**

Pivot joint

Pivot joints consist of the rounded end of one bone fitting into a ring formed by the other bone. Such a structure allows rotational movement, as the rounded bone moves around its own axis. An example of a pivot joint is the joint in the forearm allowing the radius and ulna to rotate. Another example is the first and second vertebrae of the neck that allow the head to rotate back and forth.

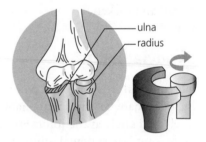

Figure 2.5 **The pivot joint**

Exam tip

You may need to identify major bones on a drawing of a skeleton.

Typical mistake

Students regularly mistake the knee for the wrong type of synovial joint. It is a hinge (synovial) joint.

Now test yourself

TESTED ☐

1 What type of joint is the knee?
2 What type of joint is the shoulder?
3 What type of joint is the hip?
4 What type of joint is the ankle?

Exam practice

1 Identify the type of joint in the knee. Tick **one** box only. [1]
  a pivot joint ☐
  b hinge joint ☐
  c ball and socket joint ☐
  d gliding joint ☐
2 Analyse the movements that take place at a ball and socket joint of your choice. (Eduqas only) [5]
3 Identify **four** features of a synovial joint. [4]

ONLINE ☐

Function of the skeletal system

The major functions of the skeletal system include:

- **Movement**: the bones act as anchor points for the muscles to attach to. The muscles can contract and pull on the bones, causing movement.
- **Support**: as the bones are relatively solid and rigid, they keep the body upright and hold major organs and muscles in place.
- **Protection**: the bones act as a guard or casing for the major organs. For example, the skull encases the brain and the ribs protect the vital organs – the heart and lungs.
- **Production of blood cells**: the inner marrow of long bones produces red and white blood cells. The red cells carry oxygen and the white cells fight infection.

> **Antagonistic pairs**: the action of one muscle contracting while its partner muscle relaxes.

> **Typical mistake**
>
> Students often confuse an upward movement of an extended arm at the shoulder. This is flexion, whereas the downward movement is extension.

> **Exam tips**
>
> You can create your own way to remember the functions of the skeleton, but here is one example of a statement: 'Support the movement to protect blood cells'.
>
> You can remember adduction as it adds to the midline of the body.
>
> The muscle causing the movement is called the agonist and the muscle relaxing as a result is called the **antagonist**.

The Eduqas specification specifically states that students must be aware of flat bones that provide protection:

- The cranium protects the skull.
- The ribs and sternum protect the vital organs – the heart and lungs.

The skeleton's role in movement allows different actions to take place at joints. It is important that you can identify examples of flexion and extension, adduction and abduction, and circumduction and rotation.

Flexion and extension

In the elbow, the biceps cause flexion whereas the triceps cause extension.

In the knee, flexion (bending) is caused by the hamstrings whereas extension is caused by the quadriceps.

Hip flexors cause flexion at the hip whereas extension is caused by the gluteals.

Flexion and extension at the ankle are slightly different in that the closing of the joint angle is called dorsiflexion, caused by the tibialis anterior. The opening of the angle is called plantar-flexion, caused by the gastrocnemius.

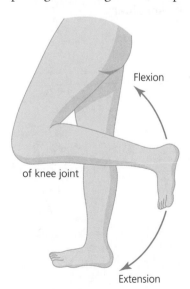

Flexion

of knee joint

Extension

Figure 2.6 Flexion is generally where the angle of a joint closes, whereas extension sees the angle open. At the knee, the hamstrings cause flexion whereas the quadriceps cause extension

Adduction and abduction

Adduction involves movement towards the midline of the body whereas abduction is movement away. At the shoulder, abduction is caused by the deltoid muscle. Adduction involves the latissimus dorsi and the pectoral muscles. Abduction and adduction can also occur at the hip.

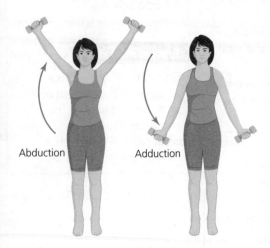

Abduction   Adduction

Figure 2.7 Adduction and abduction of the shoulder

Circumduction and rotation

Circumduction is a mixture of flexion, extension, adduction and abduction so that the extended arm moves in a cone-like formation. It occurs at the shoulder, hip and wrist.

Rotation (Figure 2.8) can be internal or external and involves the use of the rotator cuff muscles at the shoulder.

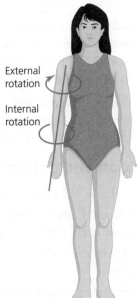

External rotation

Internal rotation

Figure 2.8 Rotation of the shoulder

> **Revision activity**
>
> In pairs, take turns at stating a movement for the other person to physically demonstrate before swapping roles. Try to name the muscles causing the movements.

Now test yourself

TESTED ☐

1 What is flexion?
2 What is extension?
3 What is abduction?
4 What is adduction?
5 What movements can occur at the elbow?

Exam practice

1 Classify the types of movement the ball and socket at the shoulder joint is capable of. Tick **one** box only.   [1]
   a flexion   ☐
   b extension   ☐
   c abduction   ☐
   d all of the above ☐
2 Identify the **four** major functions of the skeleton.   [4]
3 Explain how flexion and extension occur at the knee.
   (Eduqas only)   [2]

ONLINE ☐

Structure of the muscular system

The body contains a large number of muscles. The primary role of muscles is to attach to bones to initiate movement. However, there are different types of muscle in the body.

Skeletal muscles are attached to the bones on the skeleton, and provide movement of the body. The muscles contract, enabling the bones to be pulled. They only contract when told to by the brain and therefore they are deemed **voluntary muscles**. Skeletal muscles also help to hold bones in place and maintain posture.

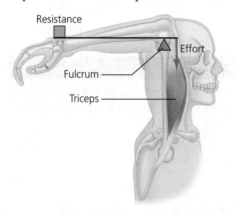

Figure 2.9 The triceps attached to the skeleton

Many of the main muscles of the body can be associated with sporting movements. For example:
- biceps cause flexion of the arm at the elbow
- triceps cause extension of the arm at the elbow
- quadriceps cause extension of the leg at the knee
- hamstrings cause flexion of the leg at the knee.

Smooth muscle is found in the wall of our internal organs such as the digestive system and helps body functions to occur. These functions occur without conscious control and are therefore deemed **involuntary muscles**.

Cardiac muscle is muscle that is involuntary and found in the walls of the heart. This type of muscle only exists in your heart and unlike other types of muscle, never gets tired. It works automatically (involuntary) and constantly without ever stopping to rest.

> **Skeletal muscles**: attach to the skeleton to cause movement.
>
> **Voluntary muscles**: under conscious control.
>
> **Smooth muscle**: found inside hollow organs to maintain body functions.
>
> **Involuntary muscles**: work without subconscious control.
>
> **Cardiac muscle**: found in the wall of the heart.

Exam tip

Remember that the main type of muscle for **movement** is **skeletal** muscle. You can remember this by the fact it attaches to the **skeleton** to cause **movement**.

Revision activity

Revise the role of the main skeletal muscles by performing an action and stating out loud what muscle/s caused the movement.

Typical mistake

It is a common mistake to assume that the cardiac muscle is voluntary. It is not.

Now test yourself

TESTED

1 What is skeletal muscle?
2 What is smooth muscle?
3 What is cardiac muscle?

Exam practice

1 Identify the type of muscle that the triceps is an example of. Tick **one** box only. [1]
  a skeletal muscle ☐
  b smooth muscle ☐
  c involuntary muscle ☐
  d none of the above ☐
2 Identify **two** features of cardiac muscle. [2]

ONLINE

Muscle fibre types

The varying muscles of the body are important in allowing movement to take place. They are attached to bones by tendons. Bones attach to other bones with ligaments. As a muscle contracts, it pulls on a bone, causing movement.

Inside each muscle, there are two different types of **muscle fibre**:

- slow twitch type I fibres
- fast twitch type II fibres.

It is important to identify the characteristics and functions of each muscle fibre type as shown in Table 2.1.

> **Muscle fibre type**: refers to the type of muscle fibre. It can be slow twitch type I or fast twitch type II.

Table 2.1 The characteristics and functions of muscle fibres

Fibre type	Characteristics	Function
Slow twitch type I	• Make use of oxygen • Energy provided aerobically • Small amounts of power • Highly resistant to fatigue • High levels of red blood cells, mitochondria, myoglobin, etc. • Relatively slow contraction speed	For events that are aerobic and at a relatively low intensity so that fatigue is not a problem.
Fast twitch type II	• Work anaerobically • Limited to no use of oxygen • High amounts of power created • Low resistance to fatigue • Low levels of red blood cells, mitochondria, myoglobin, etc. • Quick contraction speed	For fast, powerful events where fatigue happens quickly.

A   B   C

Figure 2.10 A sprinter leaving the blocks would make use of their fast twitch type II fibres.

> **Exam tip**
>
> It is important that you can identify activities that make use of slow twitch type I fibres or fast twitch type II fibres. Try to stick to extreme examples, such as marathon running for slow twitch and sprinting for fast twitch.

Exam practice

1 Explain why fast twitch muscle fibre type fatigues quickly. (Eduqas only) [2]
2 Outline two physiological differences between a fast and a slow twitch muscle fibre. (Eduqas only) [2]
3 Identify which muscle fibre type is most likely to be used by a 60m indoor sprinter. Give a reason for your answer. [2]
4 Explain the importance of fast twitch fibres to a performer when playing a team game such as rugby. (Eduqas only) [4]

ONLINE

Now test yourself

1 Name the two muscle fibre types.
2 Which muscle fibre type creates power and fatigues quickly?
3 Which muscle fibre type fatigues slowly?

TESTED

Cardio-respiratory and vascular systems: structure

The cardio-respiratory and vascular systems are in fact slightly different things. **Cardiovascular** refers to your heart, blood vessels and blood. **Cardio-respiratory** includes all of the cardiovascular system and your breathing apparatus, too.

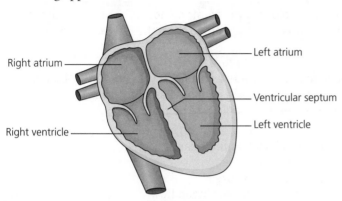

Right atrium — Left atrium

Ventricular septum

Right ventricle — Left ventricle

Figure 2.11 Basic structure of the heart

As you can see, the heart is a double pump with two sides. The left-hand side of the heart (right as you look at it) involves blood entering the left atrium from the lungs (oxygenated blood). The blood is passed through to the left ventricle and then pumped out to the working muscles. The ejection pressure of this contraction is known as systole. A normal systole is 120 mmHg.

The right side of the heart (left as you look at it) deals with deoxygenated blood from the body, which enters the right atrium, is passed through to the right ventricle and then pumped to the lungs to be oxygenated.

Valves prevent backflow of blood when moving from atria to ventricles and when leaving the arteries.

The pulmonary and systemic circulatory systems

Table 2.2 The pulmonary and systemic systems

Pulmonary system	Systemic system
● **Pulmonary circulation** only occurs between the heart and the lungs. ● Pulmonary circulation involves the circulation of blood in which **deoxygenated** blood is pumped from the heart to the lungs via the pulmonary artery. ● **Oxygenated** blood is also returned back to the heart via the pulmonary vein.	● **Systemic circulation** only occurs between the heart and the body. ● Systemic circulation involves the circulation of blood in which **oxygenated** blood is pumped from the heart to the body via the aorta. ● **Deoxygenated** blood is returned back to the heart via the vena cavae.

> **Cardiovascular**: refers to your heart, blood vessels and blood.
>
> **Cardio-respiratory**: the cardiovascular system and breathing apparatus.
>
> **Pulmonary circulation**: occurs between the heart and the lungs.
>
> **Systemic circulation**: occurs between the heart and the body.

> **Exam tip**
>
> Remember that the **systemic** circulation system feeds all of the body's **systems** with oxygenated blood.
>
> Also remember that resting heart rate tends to be 60–90 beats per minute. The average is 72 beats per minute. Training can increase the size of the heart, causing resting heart rate to lower.

Exam practice

1 Describe the route of blood from the lungs to the body. [6]
2 Identify where in the vascular system oxygenated blood will be found. Tick **one** box only. [1]

    a   arteries ☐
    b   left ventricle ☐
    c   pulmonary vein ☐
    d   all of the above ☐

ONLINE ☐

Now test yourself

1 What is the systemic circulatory system?
2 What is the pulmonary circulatory system?
3 What are the main chambers of the heart called?

TESTED ☐

Cardio-respiratory and vascular systems: blood vessels

Blood is carried via blood vessels. There are different types of blood vessels with different functions. These are shown in Table 2.3

Table 2.3 The functions of different blood vessels

Arteries	<ul><li>**Arteries** carry blood away from the heart. The biggest artery is the aorta, which carries blood from the left ventricle to the body.</li><li>Blood is under high pressure.</li><li>They have muscular walls and a narrow diameter for blood. This allows the arteries to change diameter to vasoconstrict (close) or vasodilate (open). (See page 33.)</li></ul>
Veins	<ul><li>**Veins** carry blood back to the heart.</li><li>Thinner walls than arteries.</li><li>Blood under lower pressure.</li><li>Larger internal diameter for blood flow.</li></ul>
Capillaries	<ul><li>**Capillaries** are tiny, thin walled structures (1-cell thick).</li><li>Allow for diffusion of gas.</li></ul>

Revision activity

Try to draw a cross-sectional drawing of an artery, vein and capillary, labelling the size of the walls and diameter of the internal space for blood flow (lumen).

Arteries: carry blood away from the heart under high pressure.

Veins: carry blood back towards the heart under relatively low pressure.

Capillaries: very thin structures, which allow gas exchange.

Exam practice

1 Identify **three** main characteristics of an artery. [3]
2 Which of the following characteristics describes a vein?
   Tick **one** box only. [1]
   a   high pressure blood flow ☐
   b   small lumen ☐
   c   carry blood back to the heart ☐
   d   allow gas exchange ☐
3 Fill in the table below to show the main characteristics of an artery and a capillary. [3]

Blood vessel	Pressure	Wall size	Lumen diameter
Artery			Small
Capillary	Low	Very thin	

ONLINE

Exam tip

Remember that **a**rteries carry blood **a**way from the heart.

Now test yourself

1 What is an artery?
2 What is a vein?
3 What is a capillary?
4 What are their functions?

TESTED

Cardio-respiratory and vascular systems: functions of blood vessels

The previous section has shown the basic functions of blood vessels. It is however important to fully understand the role of blood vessels in relation to the transportation of nutrients, oxygen and waste products, thermoregulation, vasodilation and vasoconstriction.

Transportation of nutrients

The main concept to understand is that oxygen that has been breathed in needs to be transported to the working muscles to allow energy to be made for movement. Equally, waste products like carbon dioxide must be removed, by being breathed out or converted into water.

Thermoregulation

Thermoregulation involves the body regulating temperature, making use of the thermoregulatory centre in the brain. Thermoreceptors monitor the temperature within the body and inform the thermoregulatory centre.

Hot conditions

If the body is too hot, blood is taken closer to the skin, making it appear red. As well as losing heat through the evaporation of sweat, arteries that run near to the skin **vasodilate** (open up) to allow more blood through. This allows heat to be lost via radiation (infrared rays) and convection, meaning heat is lost into the air.

Cold conditions

If the body is too cold, blood is taken away from the skin. As well as involuntary shivering to keep you warm, arteries that run near to the skin **vasoconstrict** (start to close up) to prevent as much blood moving through. This prevents heat loss and ensures blood is supplied to the body's core and vital organs, such as the lungs and liver.

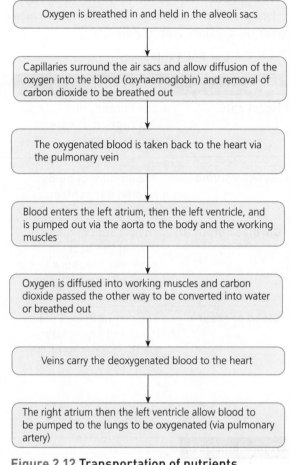

Figure 2.12 Transportation of nutrients

Oxygen is breathed in and held in the alveoli sacs

Capillaries surround the air sacs and allow diffusion of the oxygen into the blood (oxyhaemoglobin) and removal of carbon dioxide to be breathed out

The oxygenated blood is taken back to the heart via the pulmonary vein

Blood enters the left atrium, then the left ventricle, and is pumped out via the aorta to the body and the working muscles

Oxygen is diffused into working muscles and carbon dioxide passed the other way to be converted into water or breathed out

Veins carry the deoxygenated blood to the heart

The right atrium then the left ventricle allow blood to be pumped to the lungs to be oxygenated (via pulmonary artery)

Thermoregulation: the control of temperature within the body.

Vasodilation: increasing the diameter of small arteries to increase the blood flow.

Vasoconstriction: reducing the diameter of small arteries to reduce the blood flow.

Now test yourself

TESTED

1 What is vasodilation?
2 What is vasoconstriction?
3 How does oxygen reach the working muscles?

Exam practice

1 Describe what is meant by the term thermoregulation and explain why an understanding of thermoregulation is important to an athlete training in extreme heat. [5]
2 Explain how oxygen is taken to the working muscles from the alveoli sacs. [3]
3 Describe what is meant by thermoregulation and explain how this process occurs when the body starts to exercise. [3]

ONLINE

Exam tip

Remember that a boa constrictor snake wraps around its prey and squeezes. Thus vasoconstriction involves a squeezing effect to cause the artery to narrow.

Cardio-respiratory and vascular systems: cardiac values

Cardiac values refer to the different measurements that can be taken relating to the heart. Table 2.4 names these measurements and explains what these values typically are.

Table 2.4 Cardiac values

Name	Explanation	Value
Heart rate	The number of contractions/beats per minute (bpm).	• Normal range at rest 60–90 bpm for an adult • Average at rest: 72 bpm • Maximal heart rate 220 – age • Aerobic heart rate zone: 60–80% of maximal heart rate
Stroke volume	The amount of blood ejected per contraction/beat.	• Averages 70ml per beat at rest • Averages 130ml during exercise
Cardiac output (Q)	The amount of blood leaving the heart in a minute. Measured as heart rate × stroke volume.	• Referred to as 'Q' • Averages approximately 5l per minute at rest and rises to over 20l per minute during exercise
Blood pressure	The strength exerted by the blood on the vessel walls as a result of the heart beating.	• Measured as systole divided by diastole. Systole is the highest pressure as it leaves the heart. Diastole is the lowest pressure as it enters the heart. • Typical blood pressure reading should be 120/80 • A systole of 140 or more = high blood pressure • A systole of 100 or less= low blood pressure. • It is measured in mmHg.

Typical mistake

It is a mistake to think that a high resting heart rate is a good thing. A heart rate of below 60 beats per minute is known as an 'athlete's heart'.

Now test yourself

TESTED

1 What is cardiac output?
2 What is the normal range for resting heart rate?
3 What unit is blood pressure measured in?

Exam practice

1 Identify a normal measure of blood pressure. Tick **one** box only. [1]
   a 100/80 ☐
   b 120/80 ☐
   c 125/100 ☐
   d 80/100 ☐
2 What is stroke volume and how is it affected by increases in intensity of exercise? [2]
3 A young athlete has a resting heart rate of 82 beats per minute. Twelve months later he records a resting heart rate of 58 beats per minute. Analyse this result, suggesting reasons for the change in the reading. [6]

ONLINE

Heart rate: the number of heart beats (typically in a minute).

Stroke volume: the amount of blood ejected per heart beat.

Cardiac output (Q): heart rate × stroke volume.

Blood pressure: a measurement of systolic pressure (ejection) divided by diastolic pressure (filling).

Exam tips

Systole refers to the pressure when the heart **s**quirts the blood (ejects it in a contraction).

To remember the average heart rate at rest recite: 'Seventy-two ... is normal for you.'

Cardio-respiratory and vascular systems: respiratory system

The pathway of air into the body involves many complex structures. Pressure causes the lungs to expand to take air in and as pressure builds inside, so the air is then expelled back out. During **inspiration** the chest expands and the diaphragm contracts and flattens. During **expiration** the chest volume decreases and the diaphragm relaxes and forms a dome shape.

Air initially moves in through the mouth and nose before entering the respiratory tracts – the trachea, bronchi (bronchus), bronchioles and **alveoli**. These can be seen in Figure 2.13.

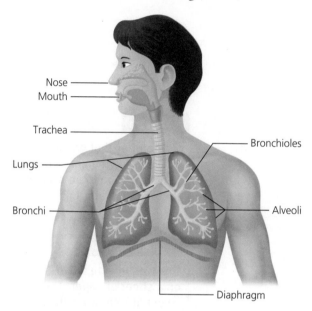

Figure 2.13 The respiratory system

As air enters the alveoli, the process of **gas exchange** takes place. As the **concentration** of oxygen is higher in the alveoli compared to the blood in the passing capillaries, oxygen moves from a high concentration to a low concentration and enters the blood stream, attaching to **haemoglobin** in the red blood cells. The oxidised haemoglobin, known as oxyhaemoglobin, travels to the heart to then be pumped around the body. As well as the oxygenation of blood, carbon dioxide moves from the red blood cells in the blood into the alveoli to be breathed out.

The alveoli are designed for gas exchange in the following ways:
- The alveoli are large in number allowing a large surface area for diffusion.
- The alveoli walls are very thin (one cell thick) allowing gas exchange to take place.
- The capillaries provide a constant blood supply for diffusion.
- The capillaries touch the alveoli walls, allowing a short diffusion pathway.

> **Exam tip**
>
> The features of the respiratory system can be remembered as an upside down tree:
> - **Tr**unk: **Tr**achea
> - **Br**anches: **Br**onchus
> - Smaller **br**anches: **Br**onchioles
> - **A** leaf: **A**lveoli

> **Inspiration**: breathing in.
>
> **Expiration**: breathing out.
>
> **Alveoli**: tiny air sacs in the lungs that allow gaseous exchange.
>
> **Gas exchange**: the process of diffusion of gas from an area of high concentration to one of low concentration.
>
> **Concentration**: the amount of something, for example, a high concentration (amount) of oxygen.
>
> **Haemoglobin**: red pigment that is attracted to oxygen in the red blood cell.

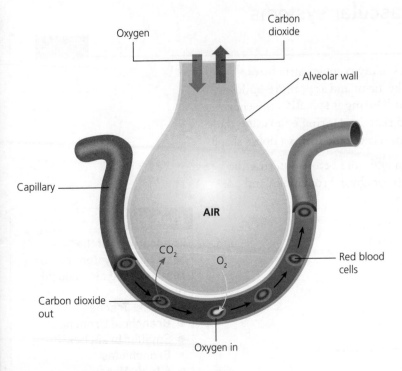

Oxygen

Carbon dioxide

Alveolar wall

Capillary

AIR

CO_2

O_2

Red blood cells

Carbon dioxide out

Oxygen in

Figure 2.14 Gas exchange at the alveoli

Now test yourself

TESTED

1 What are alveoli?
2 What is the route of air starting from the mouth and nose?
3 How does diffusion of gas occur?

Exam practice

1 Describe the route of oxygen from the atmospheric air to the working muscles. [6]
2 Explain how the characteristics of the alveoli enable gas exchange to take place. [3]

ONLINE

Exam tip

Remember that gas is diffused from an area of high concentration to an area of low concentration.

Revision activity

Draw an upside down 'Y' on a sheet of paper. The inverted Y signifies the respiratory tubes from the mouth and nose heading down into the lungs. See if you can add labels for the trachea, bronchi, bronchioles and then add the alveoli and lungs to your drawing.

Cardio-respiratory and vascular systems: lung volumes

Various lung volumes can be measured. These lung volumes include:

- **Tidal volume**: the amount of air being breathed in or out per breath.
- **Vital capacity**: the measure of maximum inspiration to maximum expiration.
- **Inspiratory reserve volume (IRV)**: the amount that can be inspired beyond tidal volume.
- **Expiratory reserve volume (ERV)**: the amount that can be breathed out beyond tidal volume.

These volumes can be measured using a spirometry trace of breathing as shown in Figure 2.2.8.

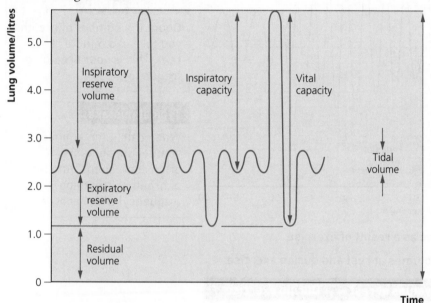

Figure 2.15 Spirometry trace of respiratory air

From a spirometry trace, you can work out the number of breaths per minute by looking at the tidal volume. Tidal volume at rest remains relatively constant and involves approximately 15 breaths per minute. As exercise starts, tidal volume increases and becomes more frequent (more breaths per minute) (see Figure 2.2.9).

As tidal volume increases, the amount left over in reserve to breathe in or out (IRV and ERV) decreases. However, the overall vital capacity remains the same.

> **Exam tip**
>
> You may need to be able to calculate 'minute ventilation'. This involves multiplying the tidal volume by the number of breaths (breathing rate in a minute).

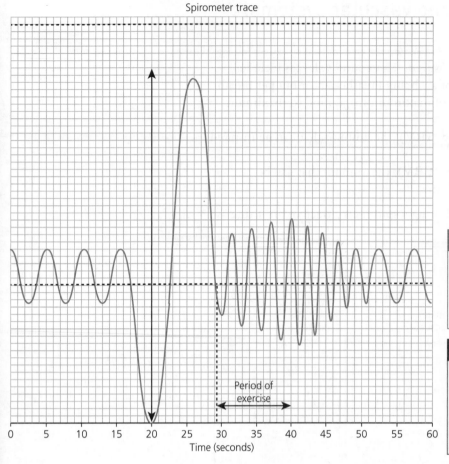

Figure 2.16 **Changes to tidal volume as a result of exercise**

Table 2.5 **Summary of breathing volumes at rest and during exercise**

Lung volume/measure	Typical values at rest	During exercise
Tidal volume	Typically ½ litre (500ml)	Increases
Vital capacity	4.5 litres	Stays the same
Breathing frequency	15 breaths per minute	Increases
Minute ventilation	6–7 litres per minute	Increases
Reserve volumes (IRV and ERV)	IRV 3.1 litres ERV 1.2 litres	Decreases

The intensity of exercise will determine the changes to lung volumes. Men and women tend to have different lung volume measures as men's lung volumes tend to be a higher.

Exam practice

1 Breathing frequency per minute × tidal volume is known as: [1]
   a   vital capacity ☐
   b   minute ventilation ☐
   c   inspiratory reserve volume ☐
   d   expiratory reserve volume ☐
2 Describe what happens to 'tidal volume' and 'vital capacity' as result of exercise. [2]

ONLINE ☐

Now test yourself

1 What is meant by tidal volume?
2 What happens to tidal volume as a result of exercise?
3 How do you calculate minute volume?

TESTED ☐

Aerobic and anaerobic exercise

Aerobic exercise occurs at a low to moderate intensity (for example, walking, jogging) when energy for exercise can be made using sufficient levels of oxygen. Aerobic exercise basically means that the body has enough oxygen to meet the energy demand.

Anaerobic exercise occurs at higher intensities (for example, powerful activities, sprinting) when energy for exercise cannot be made using sufficient levels of oxygen. Anaerobic exercise basically means that the body does not have enough oxygen to meet the energy demand.

Immediate energy demands (0–12 seconds)

When energy is needed immediately, **adenosine triphosphate (ATP)** stores in the body are used. ATP stores only last approximately 3 seconds before they need to be resynthesised. **Creatine phosphate** is an organic, energy-rich compound found in the body. When it is broken down it can re-make ATP for up to 10 seconds and becomes a valuable source of energy. ATP and creatine phosphate are therefore used for activities like javelin, discus and 100m sprinting.

10 seconds–3 minutes

After 10 seconds, if the body still requires energy it makes use of the **lactic acid** energy system. This involves the breakdown of glycogen (sugars from food). Glycogen is broken down to glucose and then pyruvic acid, but without enough oxygen, this anaerobic process results in the production of lactic acid.

3 minutes plus

For the body to exercise longer than 3 minutes it must work at a low enough intensity to be aerobic, that is, there is enough oxygen.

Anaerobic threshold and oxygen debt

Activities that involve differing intensities will vary between being aerobic and anaerobic, depending upon what the performer is doing. For example, a light jog may be aerobic whereas a sprint would be anaerobic. Every performer has a point at which the oxygen supply is not meeting the demands of the exercise and lactic acid starts to be made in higher quantities. This is known as the **anaerobic threshold** point. When there is insufficient oxygen, this is known as an oxygen deficit. After exercise an **oxygen debt** must be repaid through the process of recovery.

Aerobic exercise: exercise in the presence of enough oxygen.

Anaerobic exercise: exercise without enough oxygen.

Adenosine triphosphate (ATP): a molecule that provides energy within the cell.

Creatine phosphate: energy-rich organic compound that provides high levels of energy.

Lactic acid: compound produced when glycogen is broken down without enough oxygen being present.

Anaerobic threshold: the point during exercise at which lactic acid starts to significantly increase.

Oxygen debt: the additional oxygen that must be taken into the body after exercise to restore all systems to their normal states.

Typical mistake

Students often confuse the term **oxygen deficit** for insufficient oxygen during exercise. The process of breathing heavily during recovery involves repaying an **oxygen debt**.

Exam practice

1 Which of the following is most likely to be an aerobic event?
   Tick **one** box only. [1]
   a 100m ☐
   b 400m ☐
   c 400m hurdles ☐
   d 5000m ☐

2 Describe what is meant by the term anaerobic threshold and explain why an understanding of anaerobic threshold is important to athletes. [5]

3 Explain whether a game of football is mostly an aerobic or an anaerobic sport. Give reasons for your answer. [6]

ONLINE

Now test yourself

1 What is aerobic exercise?
2 What is anaerobic exercise?
3 When does anaerobic threshold occur?

TESTED

The characteristics and factors affecting aerobic/anaerobic exercise

The main determinant in whether an activity is aerobic or anaerobic is the amount of oxygen available for energy production in the body. However, this can be further analysed as the amount of oxygen available is determined by many factors, including:

- the **intensity** of the exercise
- the **duration** of the exercise
- the nutrients available for fuel and recovery.

> **Intensity**: how hard/how much effort is needed to perform the activity.
>
> **Duration**: how long the activity takes.

Intensity

In simple terms:

- Low to medium intensity exercise tends to be aerobic.
- High intensity exercise tends to be anaerobic.

However, the point at which an athlete starts to work anaerobically will depend on their fitness levels and ability to consume oxygen. Performers who have performed aerobic training will be likely to consume more oxygen due to physiological adaptations of training. These include making more capillaries (which wrap around alveoli) and mitochondria (where oxygen is used to make energy).

Duration

In simple terms:

- Long duration activities tend to be aerobic as, to work for such a long time, the intensity tends to be low to medium.
- Short duration activities are often explosive and high intensity, meaning that they tend to be anaerobic.

Nutrients

In simple terms:

- Low intensity aerobic events make use of fat and carbohydrates (glycogen).
- High intensity anaerobic events make use of creatine phosphate and carbohydrates (glycogen).

> **Typical mistake**
>
> Students often suggest that long aerobic events make use of fats only. They make use of carbohydrates and fats.

Table 2.6 Application of knowledge regarding intensity, duration and nutrients

Activity	Intensity	Duration	Nutrients
100m (anaerobic)	High	Short	Creatine phosphate/ glycogen
400m (anaerobic)	High	Short	Creatine phosphate/ glycogen
Marathon (aerobic)	Low	Long	Fat and glycogen
Hockey (mostly aerobic, some anaerobic)	Long	Mixed	Fat and glycogen Creatine phosphate (sprints)

Now test yourself

1 How does intensity and duration determine whether an activity is aerobic?
2 How does intensity and duration determine whether an activity is anaerobic?
3 Fat is used for what 'type' of activity?

Exam practice

1 Describe how the intensity and duration of exercise is related to the nutrient/s used for energy supply. [3]
2 A diet containing high levels of carbohydrate could be eaten in preparation to run the 400m in less than 50 seconds. Evaluate an athlete's choice to use this diet in preparation for this event. [3]

The role of nutrients in different intensities of exercise

Table 2.7 Main roles of nutrients in exercise

Nutrient	Specific need
Carbohydrate	<ul><li>The main and preferred energy source for all types of activity (aerobic and anaerobic).</li><li>Required for high and low intensity energy.</li><li>Works as a fuel for muscular contractions, acting as the main fuel for medium to high intensity exercise (80% or higher anaerobic activity).</li><li>Particularly useful for 1 minute to 2 hours of exercise.</li><li>Provided within bread, pasta, potatoes and starch-based foodstuffs.</li></ul>
Fats	<ul><li>Also an energy source.</li><li>Required for low intensity energy (aerobic) and insulation. Low intensity is aerobic (60% or lower of maximal heart rate)</li><li>Comes in two forms: saturated fat (usually animal fat) and unsaturated fat (vegetable fat/oils).</li></ul>
Protein	<ul><li>Required for tissue growth and repair.</li><li>Has a small part to play in energy.</li><li>Provided by foodstuffs like fish, meat, eggs, dairy products and nuts.</li></ul>
Minerals	<ul><li>Required for bone growth and the maintenance of regular body functions.</li><li>Inorganic substances, e.g. calcium, are good for bone formation.</li></ul>
Water	<ul><li>Required to prevent dehydration.</li><li>Approximately 8 × 8oz glasses should be drunk in an average day.</li></ul>

Manipulation of diet

In order to prepare for long-distance events, athletes often carbo-load (eat more carbohydrate than normal). This enables the athlete to work for a long time without running out of carbohydrates.

Water intake is an essential part of an athlete's preparation before and during recovery after an event. The average man should consume approximately 2.5 litres of water a day, whereas the average woman should consume approximately 2 litres.

However, during exercise a performer should consume more – but not too much more! It is recommended that a performer should sip water at regular intervals every 20 minutes or so especially in hot weather or at high altitude. For high intensity exercise lasting more than 1 hour, sports drinks or fruit juice diluted one to one with water may help extend time until exhaustion. It is also important to rehydrate after exercise.

Performers should also avoid over-consumption of water, which can be dangerous. Hyponatremia results from over-retention of water in the body. This is where the water enters the tissue cells rather than staying in the blood.

> **Carbohydrate**: sugars stored as glycogen and broken down into glucose for energy.
>
> **Fat**: stored triglycerides, which are ready for energy use during low intensity, aerobic exercise.

Now test yourself

1 What intensity of exercise makes particular use of fats?
2 What intensity of exercise makes use of carbohydrates?
3 Why is water intake essential for exercise?

TESTED

Exam practice

1 Explain why over-consumption of water can prove to be dangerous. [2]
2 Explain why carbohydrates would probably be the main energy source used during a training session for an activity such as hockey. [4]

ONLINE

Short-term effects of exercise

When the body starts to exercise, certain changes occur that can be deemed immediate or short term.

Immediate effects include:
- The skin may start to turn red as the blood flows closer to the surface.
- Body temperature starts to increase.
- Sweat may start to be produced in larger quantities.
- Heart rate and breathing rate will start to increase.

The extent of each of the above will depend upon the type of exercise being carried out. The more intense the exercise, the more likely the factors above are likely to occur.

As exercise continues, the body starts to experience short-term effects on a variety of systems. These include:
- the muscular system
- the skeletal system
- the cardiovascular system
- the cardio-respiratory system
- the energy systems being used.

These changes are summarised in Table 2.8.

> **Typical mistake**
>
> Students often forget to match the effects of exercise to the intensity being performed.

> **Now test yourself**
>
> 1 What is the difference between the cardiovascular system and the cardio-respiratory system?
> 2 What are the immediate effects of exercise?
> 3 What are the short-term effects of exercise?
>
> TESTED

Table 2.8 Short-term effects of exercise on body systems

Body system	Short-term effects of exercise	Effect of intensity
Muscular	• Muscle elasticity increases • Increase in temperature within the muscle	• Temperature increases quicker the higher the intensity
Skeletal	• Joint mobility improves allowing easier movement	• Warm-up should improve mobility • Higher intensity exercise increases mobility quicker
Cardiovascular	• Stroke volume increases • Cardiac output increase • Heart rate increases • Blood pressure changes	• All aspects occur quicker if the intensity is higher
Cardio-respiratory	• Breathing becomes more frequent • Tidal volume increases • Minute ventilation increases	• All aspects occur quicker if the intensity is higher
Energy systems	• The production of waste products depends on energy demand	• Waste products like lactic acid are produced in higher quantities during high intensity exercise

Exam practice

1 Identify the short-term effects of exercise on the cardiovascular system. Tick **one** box only. [1]
   a heart rate increasing ☐
   b heart rate decreasing ☐
   c heart rate staying the same ☐
   d initial increase then decrease ☐
2 Identify one short-term effect of exercise on the skeletal system and one on energy systems. [2]
3 Describe three short-term effects of exercise on the cardio-respiratory system. [3]

ONLINE

Long-term effects of exercise

The long-term effects of exercise depend upon what type of exercise has been performed. Weight training, for example, will have effects on the muscular system whereas continuous training will have more pronounced effects on the cardiovascular system.

The effects of exercise generally involve **adaptation** to the body's main systems:

- the muscular system
- the skeletal system
- the cardiovascular system
- the cardio-respiratory system
- the energy systems.

The long-term effects of exercise on the body's main systems are summarised in Table 2.9.

> **Adaptation**: the changes experienced in the body's systems as a result of long-term exercise.

> **Revision activity**
>
> Print pictures of different sports performers and suggest what type of training each performer has used, justifying your choices.

Table 2.9 Long-term effects of exercise on body systems

Body system	Adaptation that occurs	Detail in relation to type of training (intensity/duration)
Muscular	• Improved tone/hypertrophy (size)	• Heavy weight, low rep increases size • Low weight, high reps increases tone and muscular endurance
Skeletal	• Bone density increases	• High intensity – impact on density increases
Cardiovascular	• Hypertrophy of left ventricle • Improved ability to utilise oxygen, e.g. capillarisation of muscles and lungs causing more O_2 to diffuse	• Continuous, fartlek or interval (endurance) aerobic training causes significant adaptations
Cardio-respiratory	• Increased vital capacity • Increased efficiency e.g. increase in minute ventilation – get more O_2 into the body and remove more CO_2	• Improvement is most pronounced when working in the aerobic training zone: 60–80% of maximum heart rate, working at steady state for prolonged period of time
Energy systems	• Ability to withstand lactic acid • Ability to remove more lactic acid, therefore delaying fatigue	• Anaerobic threshold work (sprints with little rest) improves lactic acid tolerance

It can also be argued that there is a long-term psychological effect. As exercise improves self-esteem, body image and potentially results in better overall health (mental, physical and social), most people experience a positive adaptation psychologically.

Exam practice

1 Identify the most likely combination of weight-training exercises to improve muscle size. Tick **one** box only. [1]
   a heavy weights, low reps ☐
   b heavy weights, large reps ☐
   c low weights, low reps ☐
   d low weights, high reps ☐
2 Describe the use of long-term training to adapt the cardio-respiratory system for fitness. [2]

ONLINE

Now test yourself

1 How would long-term cardiovascular training affect a person's use of energy systems?
2 If light weights were used long term, what would happen to the muscles?
3 What does hypertrophy mean?

TESTED

Effects of exercise on health and well-being

The effects of exercise on social and mental well-being were outlined earlier. By means of a reminder, these points have been included in Figure 2.4.2. However, it is also important to apply these points to the performer, in relation to their training and exercise.

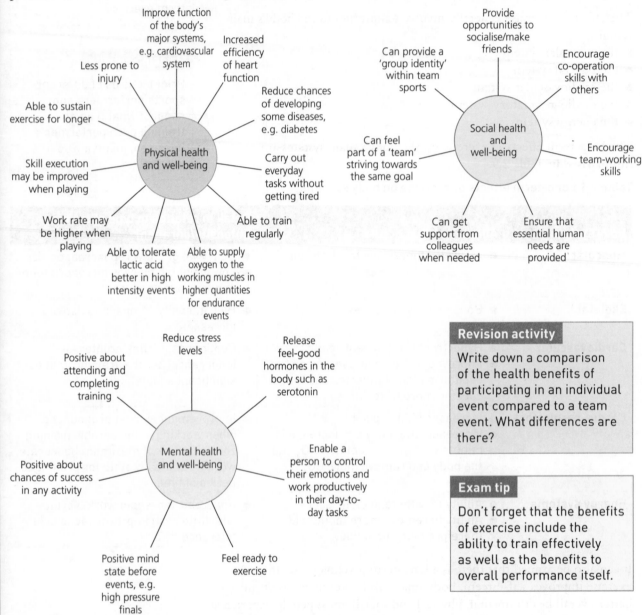

Figure 2.17 **The benefits of exercise to the performer**

Revision activity

Write down a comparison of the health benefits of participating in an individual event compared to a team event. What differences are there?

Exam tip

Don't forget that the benefits of exercise include the ability to train effectively as well as the benefits to overall performance itself.

Now test yourself

TESTED

1 Name one physical benefit of exercising.
2 Name one mental benefit of exercising.
3 Name one social benefit of exercising.

Exam practice

1 Outline **two** ways, other than meeting people, in which exercise can positively impact the social health aspects of a performance. (Eduqas only) [2]
2 Evaluate the importance to mental health and well-being of taking part in regular exercise. [4]

ONLINE

Data analysis

As a reminder, you need to be able to analyse pie charts and tabled data, while also being able to present line graphs and bar charts.

Weight training example

The tabled data below show the 1-rep max for a performer who is following a 10-week weight-training programme. The performer recorded their 1-rep max on their biceps performing an arm curl.

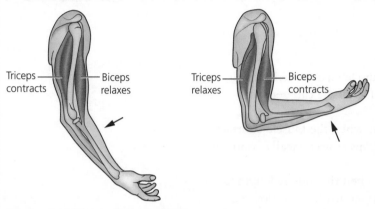

Figure 2.18 **The action of a biceps curl**

1 Analyse the data in Table 2.10. The overall improvement in 1-rep max strength has been: [1]
   a 5kg
   b 10kg
   c 15kg
   d 25kg
2 Analysing the information, state the **two** most likely adaptations of the muscular system as a result of training. [2]
3 If the performer was to continue weight training, what adaptation is likely to occur to the skeletal system? [1]
4 If the performer continued the training programme, what short-term effects would they be likely to experience during the next session? [4]

Table 2.10 **1-rep max results (biceps curl)**

Week	1-rep max test score
Week 1	15kg
Week 2	15kg
Week 3	18kg
Week 4	18kg
Week 5	20kg
Week 6	20kg
Week 7	22kg
Week 8	22kg
Week 9	22kg
Week 10	25 kg

Physiological analysis example

A group of athletes has had a physiological analysis done of their muscle fibre composition. This involves a measurement of the percentage of fast and slow twitch fibres each participant's body contains.

The results are shown in Figure 2.19.

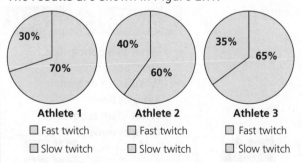

Figure 2.19 **Muscle fibre composition results**

1 Analyse the data in the pie charts to suggest who is most likely to be:
   a a discus thrower
   b a sprinter
   c a 10,000m runner [3]
2 Give reasons for your answers to Question 1. [3]
3 For the athlete you believe to be a discus thrower, do you think they could easily turn into a sprinter? Justify your answer. [3]

3 Movement analysis

Muscle contractions: isotonic and isometric

There are two types of muscle contraction:
- isotonic
- isometric.

An isotonic contraction occurs when the muscle changes length as it contracts to cause movement. The length of a muscle can get shorter (concentric) or longer (eccentric).

- **Concentric/isotonic** contractions occur when the muscle contracts and shortens. An example is when the biceps concentrically contracts to cause flexion at the elbow.
- **Eccentric/isotonic** contractions occur when the muscle lengthens as it contracts. This is usually associated with controlling or slowing down a movement. When the biceps concentrically contracts to cause flexion at the elbow, the triceps eccentrically contracts (lengthens) to control the movement.
- **Isometric** contractions involve the muscle contracting but staying the same length. For example, this may be to hold a balance or remain in a press-up position.

> **Exam tip**
>
> Try to remember that isotonic contractions can be concentric *or* eccentric.

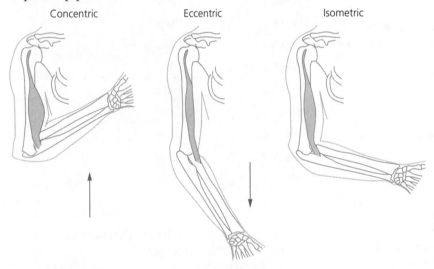

Concentric   Eccentric   Isometric

Figure 3.1 Flexion and extension at the elbow

> **Revision activity**
>
> Practise your knowledge by 'doing and saying'. Do or hold a movement and say which muscles are contracting isotonically or isometrically.

> **Typical mistake**
>
> It is a common mistake to forget to write whether a contraction is concentric or eccentric. It is more detailed to include this rather than simply stating isotonic.

Exam practice

1 Which of the following describes an isometric contraction? Tick **one** box only. [1]
   a shortening of the muscle ☐
   b isotonic contraction ☐
   c lengthening of the muscle ☐
   d held contraction length ☐
2 Analyse the contraction of muscles that takes place in the upwards and downwards phase of a biceps curl. [3]

ONLINE ☐

Now test yourself

1 What is a concentric contraction?
2 What is an eccentric contraction?
3 What is an isometric contraction?

TESTED ☐

Muscle contractions: antagonistic muscle action

Muscles work in pairs to act on a joint. As one muscle pulls the bone to cause movement, the other is able to pull the bone in the opposite direction. As one muscle contracts, the other relaxes (and vice versa). This is known as antagonistic muscle action.

One example of this is at the elbow. In basic terms during the upwards phase of a biceps curl, the biceps contracts (concentrically), allowing the arm to flex (bend). Thus the biceps is the agonist or the prime mover – the muscle causing the movement. At the same time the triceps will be relaxing as the antagonistic partner.

The movement of **antagonistic pairs** can be seen in Figure 3.2.

Figure 3.2 The movement of antagonistic pairs

In Figure 3.2:
- Picture C to D shows flexion at the elbow. The biceps is the agonist and the triceps the antagonistic partner.
- Picture A shows the arm extended. This has occurred due to concentric contraction of the triceps (the agonist). The biceps will have relaxed as the antagonistic partner.
- Picture C to D shows extension of the leg at the right knee. The agonist is the quadriceps, which have concentrically contracted to cause the flexion. The hamstrings have acted as the antagonist.

> **Antagonistic pair**: muscles that work as pairs to do the opposite to each other.

> **Revision activity**
>
> Work in pairs. Choose a sporting movement that occurs at the elbow, knee or hip. Explain to a revision partner how this movement takes place and what muscle/s are the antagonistic pairs.

> **Typical mistake**
>
> It is a common error to rush questions on muscles that have caused movement. Time should be taken to decipher what movement is taking place and how it occurs.

Exam practice

1 Complete the table to show the type of muscle contraction, the main agonist and the joint action occurring at the knee when performing the phases of a squat. [3]

	Type of contraction	Main agonist	Joint action
Upwards phase	Concentric	Quadriceps	
Downwards phase			Flexion

2 Complete the table to show the type of muscle contraction, the main agonist and the joint action occurring at the ankle when performing the phases of a squat. [3]

	Type of contraction	Main agonist	Joint action
Upwards phase		Gastrocnemius	
Downwards phase	Eccentric		Dorsiflexion

ONLINE

> **Now test yourself**
>
> 1 What is an agonist muscle?
> 2 What are antagonistic pairs?
>
> TESTED

Lever system

Levers are made of three basic parts: the fulcrum/pivot, the effort and the load. The fulcrum/pivot provides a fixed point about which a movement takes place. The effort shows the force that causes the movement and the load acts against the force of the effort.

It is important that you can link each classification of lever to practical examples and the mechanical advantage involved in the movement.
A summary of examples is provided in Table 3.1.

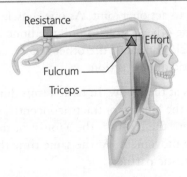

Figure 3.3 The first class lever system at the elbow joint

Table 3.1 Classification of levers and examples

Classification of lever	Diagram	Practical example	Mechanical advantage
First class lever	Load arm / Resistance / Effort / Fulcrum / Effort arm	● Triceps extension at the elbow	● Effort arm is comparatively small therefore advantage is low
Second class lever	Load arm / Effort Resistance / Effort arm	● Plantar flexion at the ankle	● Largest effort arm. Larger effort arm than resistance arm therefore mechanical advantage is high
Third class lever	Load arm / Resistance / Effort / Fulcrum / Effort arm	● Other movements including upwards phase of a biceps curl/ shoulder movement and knee movement, e.g. flexion of the knee when running ● Hamstrings create the effort, the lower leg the load, and the hinge joint at the knee the fulcrum	● Resistance arm is bigger than effort arm therefore advantage is low

Mechanical advantage is calculated by dividing the length of the effort arm by the length of the resistance arm. Thus you can see that the second class lever has the longest effort arm, longer than the resistance arm. This allows the second class lever (at the ankle) to have the highest mechanical advantage.

As a first class lever has the longest resistance arm (compared to the small effort arm), it has the lowest mechanical advantage. This is sometimes called mechanical disadvantage.

Revision activity

1 Name and draw the lever system operating during the following movements:
   a upwards phase of a biceps curl
   b throwing a football during a 'throw in'
   c rising onto toes to reach high for a basketball shot
   d bending knee (flexion) to then kick a football
   e abduction of the shoulder

Exam tip

Remember you can assist your knowledge by using the rhyme:

1, 2, 3 ...F, L, E
- Thus a first class lever has an F in the middle.
- A second class lever has an L in the middle.
- A third class lever has an E in the middle.

Now test yourself

TESTED ☐

1 What is the rhyme to remember the middle points of a lever?
2 Name where a first class lever can be found in the body.
3 Name where a second class lever can be found in the body.
4 Name where a third class lever can be found in the body.

Typical mistake

Students often suggest that movement at the elbow is a third class lever. However, this is only true if the arm is flexing using the biceps. If the arm is extending using the triceps then this a first class lever.

Exam practice

1 Identify the difference in the mechanical advantage of a first class and second class lever system. [2]
2 Figure 3.4 shows an athlete jumping. Identify the order of lever that has operated at the ankle, allowing the woman to jump. [1]

Figure 3.4

ONLINE ☐

Planes and axes of movement: planes

Movement can occur **in** or **along** a plane. All movements can be said to be moving in one of three planes:

- **sagittal**: forwards and backwards movement
- **frontal**: side-to-side movements
- **horizontal/transverse**: rotational/turning in certain ways.

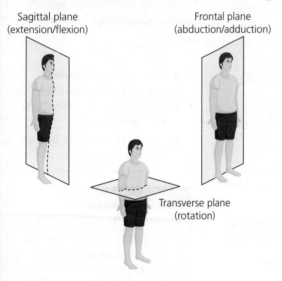

Sagittal plane
(extension/flexion)

Frontal plane
(abduction/adduction)

Transverse plane
(rotation)

Figure 3.5 The planes of movement

Using a physical activity like gymnastics you can analyse how varying movements occur in a plane. Examples include:

- sagittal plane: forward roll and somersault (forwards movements)
- frontal plane: cartwheel
- horizontal/transverse: log roll and half twist.

Now test yourself

1 What is the body doing when moving in the sagittal plane?
2 What is the body doing when moving in the frontal plane?
3 What is the body doing when moving in the horizontal/transverse plane?

Exam practice

1 Identify the plane in which running forwards in a straight line occurs. Tick **one** box only. [1]
   a   frontal plane ☐
   b   sagittal plane ☐
   c   transverse/ horizontal plane ☐
   d   all of the above ☐
2 Name the plane of movement in which a basketball player would move when performing side steps. (WJEC only) [1]
3 Evaluate how important movement in the sagittal plane is when sprinting the 100m. [3]

Exam tip

You can remember the planes of movement by using the first letter:
- **S**agittal plane divides you into **s**ides.
- **T**ransverse plane divides you into **t**op and bottom.
- **F**rontal plane divides you into **front** and back.

Typical mistake

Students often remember that the sagittal plane cuts you into sides but often mistakenly suggest it is sideways movement. Although you are cut into sides, movement **in** the sagittal plane involves forwards and backwards movements.

Revision activity

Using a sport of your choice, write down movements that occur in:
- the sagittal plane
- the frontal plane
- the horizontal/transverse plane.

Planes and axes of movement: axes

Movements occur **around** an axis. Rotating around an axis can occur in one of three ways:

- **longitudinal**: during movements in the transverse plane
- **horizontal/transverse**: during movements in the sagittal plane
- **frontal/anterior/posterior**: during movements in the frontal plane.

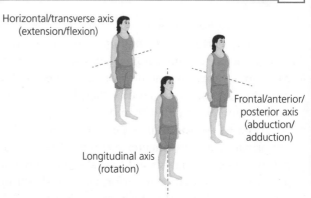

Figure 3.6 **The axes of rotation**

Exam tip

It is important that you can link your knowledge of planes and axes to movements. Remember:

- **Long**itudinal/vertical axis is the **long**est/ **V**ertical is **v**ery long
- **T**ransverse axis is like a **t**able footballer
- **Front**al axis goes in through your **front**.

Try to remember what muscles are used to carry out each movement in the tables below, for example, flexion at the arm is caused by the biceps.

Revision activity

From a team game of your choice, can you think of other examples of movement in the stated planes and around the stated axes?

Table 3.2 **Applying planes and axes to movements**

Plane	Axis	Movement	Example
Sagittal	Horizontal/ transverse	Flexion/extension	Walking, running, front somersault, flexion/ extension at the elbow when throwing, flexion/ extension at the knee when kicking a ball
Frontal plane	Frontal/anterior/ posterior	Abduction/adduction	Star jump
Horizontal/ transverse	Longitudinal/ vertical	Rotations	Ice skating spin, discus throw (rotation), rotational action when throwing cricket ball

Now test yourself

TESTED

1 What is the body doing when rotating around the longitudinal axis?
2 What is the body doing when rotating around the horizontal/ transverse axis?
3 What is the body doing when rotating around the frontal/anterior/ posterior axis?

Typical mistake

Students often confuse the names of the planes with the names of the axes. However, you must remember that movement occurs **in** a plane and **around** an axis.

Exam practice

1 Complete the table below to give examples of gymnastic movements in each of the planes. Justify your answers. [6]

Movement	Example	Justification
In the sagittal plane and around the transverse axis		
In the frontal plane and around the frontal axis		
In the transverse plane and around the longitudinal axis		

ONLINE

Sports technology for the performer

Technological advancements can play a part in preparation, analysis and recovery for a performer. **Technology** can help to improve performance. Although there are many advancements, a few examples are outlined below.

- **Monitors**: heart rate monitors, pedometers and blood pressure readers can allow an athlete to monitor their body's responses with the aim of maintaining physical health and well-being.
- **Analysis of performance**: performers can analyse aspects of performance using computer-assisted software. Cameras record performance for analysis and specialised software packages allow performers to watch their performance in slow motion or track the trajectory of objects they kick, hit or throw.
- **GPS**: GPS allows performers to monitor their movement and analyse how many metres have been run.
- **Nutrition**: software programs allow athletes to monitor their nutrition in a more detailed manner than ever before as part of their preparation for an event.
- **Equipment**: examples include footwear for footballers, clothing that reduces air resistance in cycling, and specialised prosthetic limbs for athletes with disabilities.
- **Recovery**: performers can now make use of technology to recover quicker. **Ice baths** are often used to flush the muscles with oxygen-rich blood.
- **Hyperbaric chamber**: provides a high level of oxygen and can assist with injury and rehabilitation.

Technology: any method that has been developed to improve performance.

Ice baths: a container of iced water designed to speed up recovery.

Hyperbaric chamber: high pressure chamber that increases oxygen available for recovery.

Exam tip

You can remember some of the impacts of technology on the performer by using the acronym **R MEAN**:
- **R**ecovery
- **M**onitors
- **E**quipment
- **A**nalysis of performance
- **N**utrition

Table 3.3 **Advantages and disadvantages of technology to the performer**

Advantages	Disadvantages
● Health and well-being can be monitored ● Performance can be analysed ● Nutrition can be monitored and suitably adjusted ● Greater understanding of technique being used ● Protection (equipment) ● Recover quicker	● Can be costly ● Need to know how to use the software ● May be time consuming ● May result in forcing the body to do more (if technology suggests it is possible), leading to injury

Now test yourself

1 Give one example of how technology is used for nutrition.
2 Give one example of how technology is used for recovery.
3 Give one example of how technology is used for performance analysis.

Revision activity

Using the activity you perform the most, list the different ways in which technology is used by elite level performers in that activity.

Exam practice

1 Which of the following is an example of technological being used for recovery? Tick **one** box only. [1]
   a   ice bath ☐
   b   heart rate monitor ☐
   c   GPS ☐
   d   streamlined clothing ☐
2 Describe **two** ways in which technology has improved performance as a result of sports equipment. [2]
3 Discuss the impact of technology on sports performance in a sporting activity of your choice. [6]

Typical mistake

It is a common mistake for students to suggest that technology only provides advantages to performers. There are also disadvantages (see Table 3.3).

ONLINE

Sports technology for the coach

Many of the technological advancements that can assist a performer can also assist the coach in their role to improve their athlete's performance.

Table 3.4 **Ways in which the coach can use technology**

Example of technology	How the coach can use the technology
Equipment in cricket Cricketer is given a new, state-of-the-art bat by a sponsor.	The coach could analyse where runs are scored using motion–tracking software and provide advice to the performer on how they are using the bat.
GPS in football The use of GPS allows performers to monitor their movement and to track which particular areas of a field of play they have covered.	The coach can analyse whether a performer is moving in the correct areas of the field. Players in specific positions may have been given tactics and strategies by their coach to follow. The GPS information can allow the coach to see if the performer is working hard enough and in the correct areas of the field.
Analysis of performance in triple jump Cameras record performance So that performers can analyse technique.	The coach can watch technique within performance and advise on any minor tweaks to make to the run up or jumping phases.
Heart rate monitors for cycling Heart rate monitors provide information on recorded heart rates during a race.	The coach can analyse the data and suggest if the heart is being worked in a suitable heart rate zone, working too hard or too little.
Nutrition for marathon running Software programs allow athletes to monitor their nutrition in a more detailed manner than ever before.	The coach can advise on the amount of carbohydrate being eaten. Coaches can advise on loading excess carbohydrate before a race to ensure that carbohydrate does not run out during the race.

There are advantages and disadvantages of using technology for a sports coach.

Table 3.5 **Advantages and disadvantages of using technology for a sports coach**

Positives	Negatives
<ul><li>Health and well-being of the athlete can be monitored</li><li>Performance of athlete can be analysed</li><li>Nutrition of athlete can be monitored and suitably adjusted</li><li>Greater understanding of technique being used by performer</li><li>Ensure the performer is suitably protected (equipment)</li><li>Help performer to recover quicker</li></ul>	<ul><li>Can be costly: the coach may be involved in a budget</li><li>Need to know how to use the software</li><li>May be time consuming</li><li>May prevent natural feedback from the coach who becomes reliant on technology</li><li>May misinterpret technology and provide incorrect advice</li></ul>

Exam practice

1 Which of the following is an advantage of using sports technology for a coach? Tick **one** box only. [1]
   a Can ensure performer is protected ☐
   b Can monitor health and well-being of performer ☐
   c Greater understanding of performer's technique ☐
   d All of the above ☐
2 Discuss the advantages and disadvantages of a coach using sports technology. [6]

ONLINE

Now test yourself

1 Give one example of a monitor that a coach could use with their athlete.
2 Give one example of a piece of equipment that a coach could provide their performer with to recover quicker.
3 Give one positive and one negative of sports technology for a performer.

TESTED

Sports technology for the official

Sports technology impacts greatly on sporting officials who can now make more accurate, informed decisions. The probability of 'human error' has been reduced as officials can consult technology to be certain that decisions are fair and accurate.

Technology in sport is used by officials in the following ways:
- making decisions
- measuring/scoring
- communication.

Specific examples of these are listed below:
- **Goal line technology in football**: determines whether or not the ball is over the line (in goal-scoring situations). The technology is reliable and valid, ensuring that decisions are fair.
- **TMO in rugby**: determines whether or not a try was scored.
- **Hawkeye in tennis**: players can appeal a certain number of decisions, which can be checked by officials using Hawkeye.
- **DRS in cricket**: allows play to be reviewed to see if the ball was going to hit the stumps or did hit the bat.
- **False starts in athletics**: starter blocks detect if a sprinter has started before the gun has gone.
- **Communication between officials in football**: football officials can communicate with each other via intercom headsets.

There are advantages and disadvantages for officials in using technology.

> **Exam tip**
>
> It is important that you can provide examples of how technology is used by officials.

> **TMO** (television match official): allows referees to review moments of the game in slow motion and from different angles.
>
> **Hawkeye**: technology used to track the flight path and landing point of tennis balls.
>
> **DRS** (decision review system): allows officials to review the flight path of and contact made on the cricket ball.

Table 3.6 **Advantages and disadvantages of using technology for officials**

Advantages	Disadvantages
• Decisions are fair • Removes the ability of players to manipulate the official • Takes responsibility away from the official • Some technology has proven that officials are usually correct, e.g. DRS • Prevents controversy within decision-making • Relatively quick to use • Allows decisions to be made from many angles and in slow motion • Increased objectivity (less subjectivity) in some decisions, e.g. in tennis	• Technology can be wrong • May discredit the official if it proves they were wrong • Can take time • Disrupts the flow of an event • Goes against the traditional nature of being an official • Can become over-reliant on technology • May remove the need for human officials

Now test yourself

1 Give an example from a sport of your choice of technology used to make decisions.
2 Give an example from a sport of your choice of technology used to allow communication.

Exam practice

1 Describe the impact of **one** technological development that has been introduced to support officials in sport. [2]
2 Discuss how successful support provided by technology has been for officials. [6]

ONLINE

> **Revision activity**
>
> Write down the names of five different sports and list how officials use technology to make decisions in those sports.

Cricket example

The data in the pie chart (Figure 3.7) show how a cricket team scored runs during a recent match. The areas of the pie chart correspond to named 'areas of the field'.

1 In which area of the field were most runs scored? [1]
2 In which area of the field were the least runs scored? [1]
3 Evaluate the role that technology has played for the batters in the team. How can this data help them? [3]
4 State, using **one** example, how technology can help an official in sport. [2]

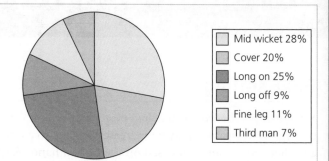

Mid wicket 28%
Cover 20%
Long on 25%
Long off 9%
Fine leg 11%
Third man 7%

Figure 3.7 **Pie chart to show distribution of runs scored by a cricket team**

Cycling example 1

The data in Table 3.7 show the highest recorded heart rates of a group of cyclists during an 80-mile race. Each cyclist wore a heart rate monitor and the highest heart rates recorded were placed in the table below.

Using graph paper, plot a line graph that shows the highest heart rates recorded for each athlete, including suitably labelled axes. [3]

Table 3.7 **Maximum heart rates recorded**

Person	Maximum heart rate recorded (to nearest 5 bpm)
1	195
2	180
3	165
4	165
5	140
6	185
7	195

Cycling example 2

The information in Figure 3.8 shows the recorded heart rate of a cyclist who has performed in a long-distance cycling event. The cyclist wore a heart rate monitor, which was linked to the watch they were wearing. Having finished the race, the cyclist decided to make use of the technological data they have recorded.

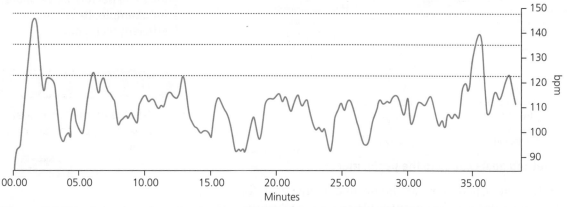

Figure 3.8 **Graph to show heart rate recorded during a long-distance event**

Help the cyclist to answer the following questions:
1 What was my highest recorded heart rate during the race? [1]
2 Explain why my heart rate was raised so much at about 35 minutes? [2]
3 Did I (the cyclist) work in my aerobic training zone? (NB: I am 25 years old.) [2]
4 If I expected to reach 80 per cent of maximal heart rate at one point in the race, did my heart rate reach this point? [1]
5 How can I explain the immediate rise in heart rate at the start of the race? [2]
6 If I want to improve my aerobic ability, what should my aerobic training zone be for training from now on? [2]

4 Psychology of sport and physical activity

Goal-setting

REVISED

Setting a specific goal can help a performer to aim towards a set purpose or target. Motivation may be increased as they strive towards that goal and their mind can be focused on the task in hand. A goal may be a performance target, such as to improve their start, or an outcome target, such as to ultimately win a race.

Setting goals can improve health and well-being, as the performer:
- may improve fitness, resulting in physical health and well-being being improved. If the goal set is based on an improvement in fitness, the performer will be able to meet their daily training demands with more ease and can use the principle of overload to push their body harder.
- may feel more focused and increase their effort, thus feeling more motivated and concentrated (mental health and well-being). If the performer knows their goal and the effort required to meet that goal, they know what they have to do and can come to terms with the demands of meeting the goal.

As an example, if a sprinter has a set goal to win the Olympic 100m final the goal itself may be rather ambitious. However, if they feel that goal is achievable it can help the performer in many ways, as shown in Figure 4.1.

Figure 4.1 Setting goals can help the performer

However, it is often inappropriate to choose an outcome goal, for example, to win, as this may be unachievable and can demotivate performers who feel that they cannot achieve their goal.

> **Goal setting:** the act of stating a target that a performer decides to aim for.

> **Exam tip**
>
> All goals should follow the principle of being SMART (see page 57).

> **Typical mistake**
>
> Students regularly choose an outcome goal, such as to win, as their example. For most performers the goal of winning may be unrealistic and they should focus on performance goals, for example, to use more efficient technique.

> **Now test yourself**
>
> 1 What is an outcome goal?
> 2 What is a performance goal?
>
> TESTED

Exam practice

1 Identify the **two** types of goal that can be set. [2]
2 Discuss how appropriate a goal set 'to win' may be for a beginner. [4]

ONLINE

As a performer moves towards their set goal they can devise further strategies for success and focus their attention on achieving one goal at a time. Their final aim/goal will nearly always be written as a SMART target.

A SMART target is:
- **S**pecific (specific to the demands of the sport/muscles used/movements involved)
- **M**easureable (it must be possible to measure whether they have been met)
- **A**ccepted (it must be accepted/agreed by the performer and the performer's coach, if they have one)
- **R**ealistic (it must actually be possible to complete the goal, i.e. they are physically capable)
- **T**ime phased (it must be set over a fixed period of time).

SMART targets allow athletes to focus, monitor progress, plan, adapt, and show success. They can also help to motivate and give direction.

> **Typical mistake**
>
> Students often incorrectly suggest that the 'A' in SMART refers to achievable.

> **Exam tip**
>
> It is possible that you will be required to evaluate the use of a SMART target within the exam. Remember there are good and bad points to setting SMART goals.

Table 4.1 Advantages and disadvantages of setting SMART goals

	Advantages	Disadvantages
Specific	Individuals within the team will know their goal and will have specific requirements/goals to aim for.	The SMART target can lead to too much focus being placed on reaching the goal.
Measurable	It is good to monitor progress as it can be measured.	It can limit creativity if there is too much measuring.
Agreed	The performer feels like they have ownership of the target, as it is something they have agreed to do.	It relies heavily on suitable levels of intrinsic motivation.
Realistic	As it is realistic, the individual has a high chance of seeing improvement and therefore may become more motivated.	
Time	The set time allows the performer to see the improvement, and prepare punctually for an event/season.	There may be increased pressure to meet the deadline.

Other points could include: overuse or inappropriate/unrealistic use of SMART can have a negative effect on motivation and make sport become too serious/goal driven rather than fun.

Exam practice

1 The acronym SMART can be used to create goals. Which of the following is denoted by the 'A' in SMART? Tick **one** box only. [1]

  a agreed ☐
  b achievable ☐
  c acceptable ☐
  d ambitious ☐

2 Explain how a gymnast competing in the Olympics could apply SMART goal-setting, also giving the goals they could set. [5]
3 Evaluate the use of SMART targets in training for a sporting event. [6]

ONLINE

Now test yourself

1 What does SMART stand for?
2 What makes a target 'specific'?

TESTED

Information processing

Information processing is the process of inputting information to make suitable decisions. There are stages to this process, as shown in Figure 4.2.

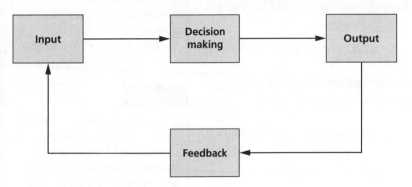

Figure 4.2 A basic information processing model

Input

- This involves taking in information from the 'display' (senses: sight, hearing, and so on).
- Then the performer will choose which sense is the most important at that given time, for example, sight when watching a netball travelling through the air. This is called selective attention – attending to the most relevant sense.

Decision making

- This is where the performer selects an appropriate response (movement/skill) from memory, perhaps one they have used in this situation before. For example, a decision to catch the netball.
- Decision making comes from the short-term memory (STM). However, the decision may have been recalled to the STM from the long-term memory (LTM).

Output

- The decision chosen is sent to the appropriate muscles to carry out the response, for example, impulses are sent to arms and hands to start the appropriate muscular movements for the catch to take place.

Feedback

- Information is received via the performer (intrinsic) and/or from other people (extrinsic).
- The feedback received may affect how you complete this skill in the future, for example, you can feel the ball in the hands (intrinsic) and your team mates cheer when you catch it (extrinsic).
- Feedback is generally grouped into technical feedback about the quality of the performance (**knowledge of performance/KP**) or about the result of the performance (**knowledge of results/KR**).

> **Knowledge of performance (KP):** detail about how well you did, relating to technique used, or specific aspects of the movement you produced. It deals with the quality of the performance, not the result.
>
> **Knowledge of results (KR):** feedback that focuses solely on how successful you have been in achieving what you set out to do (the outcome). It is generally factual and given to you by a coach or teacher, for example, what the score was, whether you did or did not score, and so on.

> **Typical mistake**
>
> Students regularly mix up knowledge of performance and knowledge of results. Remember that KR is about results, for example, did they win/score, and so on.

> **Revision activity**
>
> Write down three sporting skills and divide how the decision is made to perform these skills into input, decision making, output and feedback.

Exam practice

1 Describe the input stage of an information processing model. [2]
2 Explain, using a practical example, how information processing allows a suitable decision to be made when playing sport. [2]

ONLINE

> **Now test yourself**
>
> 1 During decision making, how is information received so it can be processed?
> 2 What is selective attention?
> 3 Where are decisions stored?
>
> TESTED

Exam practice and Data analysis answers at **www.hoddereducation.co.uk/myrevisionnotes**

Feedback is the response to the output (within information processing). Feedback can be negative or positive but holds much importance. The types of feedback are shown below:

- If feedback comes from another person it is known as '**extrinsic**'.
- If feedback comes from oneself it is known as '**intrinsic**'.
- If feedback is based on technique and performance it is called '**knowledge of performance**'.
- If feedback is based on the outcome or result it is known as '**knowledge of results**'.

Cognitive performers are more likely to respond positively to:

- positive feedback as it may keep them motivated
- extrinsic feedback as they may need help from a coach/teacher
- knowledge of results as they cannot interpret knowledge of performance.

Appropriate feedback holds significant importance as it allows a performer to know if they have been successful or not. They can therefore make any adjustments for next time. The importance of feedback can be summarised as shown in Figure 4.3.

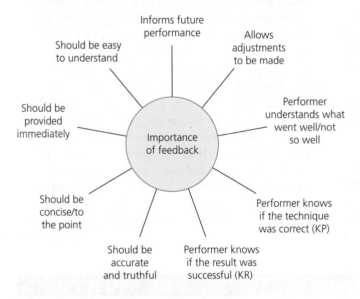

Figure 4.3 The importance of feedback

Guidance

Guidance is given by coaches or teachers to enable a performer to learn or improve. The types of guidance that can be used are:
- verbal (hearing)
- visual (seeing)
- manual (being physically moved)
- mechanical (being helped by an object/aid).

You need to know how the different types of guidance relate to the stages of learning. These are shown in Table 4.2.

Table 4.2 Types of guidance relate to the stages of learning

Stage of learning	Characteristics of the stage
Cognitive (beginner)	Inconsistent, makes mistakes, lacks fluency, uses trial and error
Associative (developing towards expert)	Understands, is becoming consistent, number of mistakes falling
Autonomous (expert)	Consistent and effective, fluent and aesthetic

- **Verbal guidance** tends to involve being told by a coach or teacher what is being done correctly or incorrectly. It is often used alongside any of the other types of guidance, for example, explaining while also being shown. It can be used at all stages of learning but should not be lengthy or complex for beginners. Autonomous performers tend to be able to interpret complex verbal guidance better than cognitive performers.
- **Visual guidance** tends to involve being shown something via a demonstration or watching video footage or still images. This may be watching yourself or another performer. Cognitive performers who are learning the skill for the first time need to be shown how the skill looks before they can understand any other type of guidance.
- **Manual guidance** tends to involve being guided physically by a coach or teacher. Examples include guiding your arm in the correct movement when playing tennis or golf, or tucking your neck in when doing a forward roll in gymnastics. Manual guidance tends to provide help, support and safety for cognitive performers, although all levels of performers may need manual guidance when stretching them to attempt something new.
- **Mechanical guidance** involves the use of aids or objects to provide safety and support. Examples include trampoline harnesses, judo belts for somersaults and armbands in swimming. The performer may well start to understand how the movement should feel but doesn't do it unassisted so it is slightly artificial. It is particularly beneficial for cognitive performers, when first learning, to encourage confidence due to the safety it provides.

Table 4.3 Guidance summary

Stage of learning	Appropriate guidance
Cognitive	- Visual - Simple verbal - May need manual and/or mechanical
Associative	- Transition between cognitive and autonomous
Autonomous	- Verbal - May need self-analysis through visual - Unlikely to need manual/mechanical

Exam practice

1 Which type of guidance are autonomous performers most likely to need? Tick **one** box only. [1]
   a manual guidance ☐
   b mechanical guidance ☐
   c visual guidance ☐
   d verbal guidance ☐
2 Identify and explain how visual, verbal and manual guidance could be provided for a beginner in badminton. [3]

Now test yourself

1 What is verbal guidance?
2 What is visual guidance?
3 What is manual guidance?
4 What is mechanical guidance?

Exam practice and Data analysis answers at **www.hoddereducation.co.uk/myrevisionnotes**

Mental preparation

Mental preparation is a vital ingredient in sporting success. Performers may well incorporate some mental preparation into their warm-up and may use specific techniques to develop focus and confidence. Developing a suitable mental state can be known as being in the right frame of mind or being **in the zone**.

Being fully mentally prepared can help performers by:
- developing high confidence levels
- controlling emotions and arousal
- improving motivation
- improving concentration
- improving commitment levels.

Mental preparation techniques that can help to motivate and improve performance include: **imagery**, **visualisation** and **mental rehearsal**. These techniques are very similar.

> **Exam tip**
>
> Remember that imagery, mental rehearsal and visualisation are all cognitive techniques – they are done mentally in your head.
>
> You can remember the importance of mental preparation by using **CREAM**:
> - **C**oncentration (improves)
> - **R**each a high level of confidence
> - **E**motions (controlled)
> - **A**rousal levels (controlled)
> - **M**otivation levels (increase)

> **In the zone**: being in a state of flow, whereby performance appears to be effortless, the performer is concentrating, has clear goals and is totally aware of themselves and their surroundings.
>
> **Imagery**: this can be done in several ways. A performer may imagine themselves in a calming environment to reduce tension and arousal. Or it can be imagining the feeling of a movement or watching a recording of their own movement.
>
> **Visualisation**: generally this is visualising a good performance in your head.
>
> **Mental rehearsal**: picturing oneself performing the perfect performance.

Now test yourself

1 What is imagery?
2 What is mental rehearsal?

Exam practice

1 Which of the following is the most accurate description of mental rehearsal? Tick **one** box only. [1]
   a imagining a calm place ☐
   b breathing deeply ☐
   c picturing a performance ☐
   d picturing the perfect performance ☐
2 Evaluate, using examples, the use of mental preparation techniques prior to an important sporting performance. [6]

ONLINE

> **Typical mistake**
>
> It is a mistake to suggest that mental preparation techniques can only be used at the autonomous stage of learning. They can be used at all stages of learning.

> **Revision activity**
>
> Try out one of the mental preparation techniques before taking part in a sport that you play.

Motivation

Motivation is a general drive to achieve. It involves determination and enthusiasm.

The main types of motivation are intrinsic and extrinsic, both of which have strong links to being determined and achieving sporting success.

- **Intrinsic motivation**: an inner drive to succeed. The performer is motivated to succeed for feelings of pride, accomplishment or fun and enjoyment.
- **Extrinsic motivation**: involves an outside influence or reward, for example, being motivated by a trophy, prize or monetary reward. Tangible extrinsic motivational tools are things you can touch, such as a trophy. Intangible extrinsic motivational rewards cannot be touched, such as praise from a coach.

It is generally accepted that intrinsic motivation is stronger than extrinsic as the feeling of wanting to achieve pride or satisfaction outweighs the desire to win extrinsic rewards. However, this is not the case for everyone and the desire to earn money or a trophy may well be a powerful motivator.

Figure 4.4 Motivational strategies

Exam practice

1 Which of the following is an example of a tangible extrinsic motivator? Tick **one** box only. [1]
   a praise from coach ☐
   b goals set by coach ☐
   c feedback from coach ☐
   d trophy from coach ☐
2 Explain, using an example, what is meant by the term intrinsic motivation. [2]
3 Evaluate, using examples, a coach's use of tangible extrinsic reward as a form of motivation for a sports performer. [4]

ONLINE ☐

Motivation: the drive to succeed or the desire to want to achieve something.

Intrinsic motivation: the drive that comes from within oneself, for example, wanting to be proud or satisfied with the achievement.

Extrinsic motivation: the drive experienced by a performer when aiming to win a tangible or intangible reward.

Exam tip

Students often mistake tangible and intangible extrinsic motivators. Remember **t**angible motivators can be **t**ouched, for example, a **t**rophy.

Revision activity

Write down what strategies your coach has used to motivate you. Then place a bracket beside each point in your list and label each as tangible or intangible.

Now test yourself

1 What is motivation?
2 What is intrinsic motivation?
3 What is extrinsic motivation?

TESTED ☐

Characteristics of a skilled performance

A skill is something that is learned. Skills can be mental or physical. When discussing a **skilled performance**, it normally refers to a physical skill, for example, passing a ball. A 'skilled performance' in sport includes many factors and characteristics:

- fluency: the performance is fluent (not jerky)
- accuracy: the performance tends to be accurate
- aesthetic: the performance looks pleasing to watch
- consistency: the performance is consistent
- confidence: the performance is done with confidence
- control: the performance includes high levels of control
- effectiveness: the performance is effective
- efficiency: the performance uses energy efficiently
- decision making: the performance includes appropriate and intelligent decision making
- technical: the performance makes use of appropriate technique
- tactical: the performance follows appropriate tactics and strategies.

> **Skilled performance**: fluent, controlled, efficient and effective.

> **Revision activity**
>
> Write down five sporting skills and research which elite performers you believe perform these skills with fluency, efficiency and effectiveness.

> **Exam tip**
>
> Remember the characteristics of a skilled performance by using **TEAM ME**:
> - **T**echnically sound
> - **E**ffective
> - **A**ccurate
> - **M**ore consistent
> - **M**ore fluent
> - **E**fficient

Now test yourself

1 Think of one element of a skilled performance.
2 Think of another element of a skilled performance.
3 Are skilled performances usually mental or physical?

Exam practice

1 Identify the definition of a skilful performance. Tick one box only.   [1]
   a fluent   ☐
   b effective   ☐
   c efficient   ☐
   d all of the above ☐
2 Identify **five** characteristics of a skilled performance.   [5]

ONLINE

Classification of skills

In order to fully understand skills used in sport, they can be classified along a continuum. The main skills classification continuum is:

- **basic** to **complex**
- **open** to **closed**
- **self-paced** to **externally paced**.

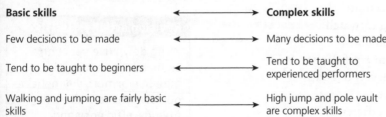

Figure 4.5 The basic to complex continuum

Open skill

Environment is unstable. Other performers affect how the skill is done. Skill is often externally paced, for example, a rugby tackle depends on what the person being tackled is doing. Passing in hockey is open.

Closed skill

Environment is stable. How you do the skill is not affected by others. Often self-paced, for example, a handstand or somersault in gymnastics. High jump is also not affected by other performers.

Self-paced skill

Start of the movement is controlled by the performer. For example, a long jump starts when you decide.

Externally-paced skill

Start of the movement is controlled by an external factor, for example, a sprint start (gun), marking an opponent in a team game.

> **Basic skill**: a skill requiring few decisions to be made.
>
> **Complex skill**: a skill requiring lots of decisions to be made.
>
> **Open skill**: a skill that is affected by the environment and people around you.
>
> **Closed skill**: a skill that is not affected by the environment and people around you.
>
> **Self-paced skill**: skill that starts when the performer decides.
>
> **Externally paced skill**: a skill that is controlled by external factors as to when it starts.

Exam tip

Be prepared to justify your decision to place a skill at a certain point on the continuum line. For example, a rugby conversion is more self-paced than externally paced as the kicker decides when to kick it and it is done in their own time. However, it may not be at the very end of the skill continuum line as they cannot take too long or the referee (external force) may intervene.

Now test yourself

1. What is meant by the open to closed continuum?
2. What is meant by the basic to complex continuum?
3. What is meant by the self-paced to externally paced continuum?

Exam practice

1. Identify a skill from a team game that can be classified as open. Justify your answer. [2]
2. Explain how a dive in swimming at the start of a race could be classified on the self-paced to externally paced continuum. [2]
3. During a gymnastics routine, a performer may perform a leap into the area and a series of cartwheels. Classify these two different movements on the basic to complex continuum, justifying your answer for both. [4]

Exam practice and Data analysis answers at **www.hoddereducation.co.uk/myrevisionnotes**

Types of practice

Coaches and sports performers will design practice sessions to enable them to improve their skills. There are different ways to structure a practice session. These include:

- whole practice
- part practice
- fixed practice
- varied practice.

> **Whole practice:** periods of practising a skill as a whole – it is not broken down.
>
> **Part practice:** periods of practising a skill in parts – it is broken up into sections.
>
> **Fixed practice:** repeating a skill in the same way over and over.
>
> **Varied practice:** changing the practice to ensure the environment is not fixed, so that the performer faces changeable and novel situations.

Different types of practice are suited to the development of different skills.

Exam tip

Remember that fixed practice should only be used with a skill that is repeated in a sporting situation without others affecting how it is done, for example, rugby conversion.

Revision activity

Start to practise the application of your knowledge. Write down five different skills from activities of your choice and decide what type of practice would be used.

Table 4.4 **The different types of practice**

Type of practice	Explanation
Whole	Involves periods of practising a skill as a whole, i.e. it is not broken down. The skill is practised in its full form without breaks. The performer has the ability to perform the whole skill as they find it relatively simple.
	Best for performers nearer to the autonomous end of the stages of learning.
	Not always appropriate for dangerous or complex skills that may be performed more safely if broken down.
Part	Involves periods of practising a skill in parts, i.e. it is broken up into sections. The skill is not practised in its full form and the parts of the skill may be practised in isolation before eventually being practised together as a whole.
	Good for performers who are relatively inexperienced (cognitive).
	Dangerous skills may be best performed in a part format to control safety.
Fixed	Repeating a skill in the same way over and over. The environment is relatively fixed and the skill is repeatable. The skill is usually 'closed', so cannot be directly affected by other performers. The skill is often 'self-paced' as the performer is in control of when they initiate the movement.
Variable	Changing the practice to ensure the environment is not fixed, so that the performer faces changeable and novel situations. The skill is often 'open', meaning it can be affected by other performers within the environment and subject to change.

Typical mistake

It is a common mistake to assume that whole practice should be used. It is only advisable if the skill is simple, safe and the performer has the ability to perform it in its whole format.

Now test yourself

1 What is whole practice?
2 What is part practice?
3 What is fixed practice?
4 What is variable practice?

TESTED

Exam practice

1 Describe the factors that would be suitable for a performer to use whole practice. [3]
2 Name a suitable practice type for a performer at the cognitive stage of learning trying a complex skill out for the first time. Justify your answer. [3]

ONLINE

Classification of skills and types of practice: applications

Practice types can be chosen to match the demands of the situation. Skills in different sporting activities require the careful selection of suitable practice types to maximise the chances of success.

Table 4.5 gives examples of sporting skills and the type of practice that is likely to suit the scenario.

> **Exam tip**
>
> Remember that 'fixed' practice is for 'fixed situations' that do not change.

Table 4.5 Examples of sporting skills and suitable types of practice

Skill situation	Type of practice
Passing in football	As passing in football is not a fixed environment, the use of **variable** practice is best. Players may well be in the way and the pass may need to go round, past or over the defender. Passing is relatively simple and not dangerous, so should be suited to a **whole** practice. Decision: whole/variable
Rugby conversion from in front of the posts	As other performers do not affect a rugby conversion, the skill can be practised using a **fixed** practice from the same spot, repeating the same action. This would allow the skill to be refined. Performers would find the skill relatively simple so could practise the **whole** skill. Decision: whole/fixed
Trampoline somersault for the first time	A trampoline somersault is a relatively dangerous skill meaning that **part** practice would be best. As the performer is a beginner, this would also lead to using part practice. However, as the skill is not affected by the environment (other performers), it can be practised in a **fixed** type of practice, repeating the skill in the same way over and over to allow refinement. Decision: part/fixed
Rock climbing for beginners	Rock climbing is extremely dangerous and tends to require **part** practice, learning how to use various techniques at a simple level first. As the group are beginners, they would be best suited to part practice. The choice to use **fixed** practice would be taken as the rock is relatively stable and the environment (other climbers) does not affect how the climb should be done. Decision: part/fixed

> **Revision activity**
>
> Look at the table above and come up with your own examples of when these practice types may be best used.

> **Typical mistake**
>
> It is a common mistake to suggest that whole practice can be used in dangerous situations.

Exam practice

1 Which of the following sets of practice types is suited to dangerous, open skills? Tick **one** box only. [1]
   a fixed, whole ☐
   b fixed, part ☐
   c variable, whole ☐
   d variable, part ☐
2 Discuss the use of different practice types in differing sporting situations. [8]

> **Now test yourself**
>
> 1 What type of practice is used for dangerous skills?
> 2 What type of practice is used for simple skills?
> 3 What type of practice is used for repeatable closed skills?
>
> TESTED

Exam practice and Data analysis answers at **www.hoddereducation.co.uk/myrevisionnotes**

Sources of motivation example

The data in the pie chart below show the main four sources of motivation for a group of sports performers.

The group was asked one simple question: 'What is the main thing that motivates you in sport?'

1 Identify the main 'source of motivation' and state whether this source is *intrinsic* or *extrinsic*. [2]
2 With reference to your answer to Question 1, explain why this may have proved to be the most popular answer. [2]
3 Identify which sources of motivation were extrinsic. [1]

4 Suggest whether intrinsic or extrinsic motivational sources tend to be more powerful. [3]

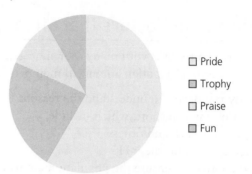

□ Pride
■ Trophy
□ Praise
■ Fun

Figure 4.6 **Pie chart to show sources of motivation for sports performers**

Skill development example

A group of GCSE PE students are trying to complete the set skill of throwing tennis balls into a bucket. Each student has 2 attempts at 10 throws. The scores achieved are shown below.

1 Identify which student gains the best average score. [1]
2 Assuming that this student shows the highest level of skill, identify three characteristics of the student's skilful performance. [3]
3 Which student do you feel demonstrates the lowest level of skill? [1]
4 Student 10 scored 7 on the first attempt and 8 on the second. They performed the full throw with the ball 10 times in each attempt. What type of practice is this? [1]
5 Turn all of the second attempts of each student into a bar chart graph using some graph paper. [6]

Table 4.6 **Number of tennis balls landing in buckets**

Student number	Attempt number 1 out of 10	Attempts number 2 out of 10
1	9	5
2	3	4
3	8	4
4	7	7
5	7	7
6	6	7
7	3	5
8	1	0
9	10	10
10	7	8

Guidance types example

1 What is the main type of guidance used with this performer? [1]
2 Explain why this guidance type was perhaps the most important. [2]
3 What can you suggest about the performer based on the mix of guidance types used? [6]

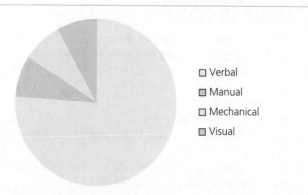

□ Verbal
■ Manual
□ Mechanical
■ Visual

Figure 4.7 **Pie chart to show guidance types used with a sports performer**

5 Socio-cultural issues in sport and physical activity

Participation: factors that affect participation

The government works with many sporting agencies to try to encourage higher rates of **participation** among all members of society.

It is firstly important to understand the reasons for trying to increase participation rates in sport, which include:
- improving health and fitness
- reducing strain on the NHS
- social control, to ensure the population are using their time to do positive things
- providing opportunities for **social interaction** and friendships, increasing social health and well-being
- maintaining a productive, fit and healthy workforce.

There are many factors that affect a person's ability to participate in sporting activities. These include:
- **Family**: a family that regularly participates in sporting activities is more likely to encourage and organise opportunities to stay active for all members.
- **Gender**: some members of society still believe that males/females should play some activities only and therefore encourage adherence to these views.
- **Society**: the government tries hard to campaign to further improve the culture of British society to ensure that taking part in physical activity is seen as the norm rather than the exception.
- **Peers**: friends and acquaintances can influence a person's decision to take part in varying activities. If a person's friends join a particular club, they are also more likely to join.
- **Access**: people can only take part in sporting activities if they are available to them. Different activities are more easily accessible in certain parts of the country than others.
- **Role models**: these can affect a person's choice of physical activity.
- **Time and money**: individuals need to manage their lives suitably to have the time to go and take part in physical activities. Similarly, many activities require a financial commitment in order to take part.

> **Participation**: the action of taking part in something.
>
> **Social interaction**: relationship between two or more people.

> **Exam tip**
>
> You can remember factors affecting participation by the term **GRAFT**:
> - **G**ender
> - **R**ole models
> - **A**ccess
> - **F**amily and friends
> - **T**ime and money

> **Typical mistake**
>
> It is a common error to suggest that all families encourage all children to take part in sporting activities.

> **Revision activity**
>
> Think about your own circumstances. How do the factors included in 'GRAFT' (see Exam tip) affect your ability to participate?

Exam practice

1 Which of the following are factors that affect the level of participation? Tick one **box** only. [1]
   a gender ☐
   b role models ☐
   c income ☐
   d all of the above ☐
2 Identify **four** factors that affect the participation rates in sport of the general public. [4]
3 Give **two** possible reasons why a female may decide not to take part in physical activity. (WJEC only) [4]

ONLINE ☐

> **Now test yourself**
>
> 1 State one factor that affects participation.
> 2 What does GRAFT stand for?
>
> TESTED ☐

Participation: factors affecting provision

The **provision of sport** refers to how sport is provided to the public. It is provided by three different sectors:

- The public sector refers to local and national government-funded **provision**. This is funded via money from taxes, with the aim of breaking even. Public sector provision includes local swimming pools and leisure centres. The quality of facilities varies considerably and may not be quite as good as the private sector.
- The private sector refers to privately run organisations that provide sporting and leisure facilities for paying members. Their aim is to provide high quality facilities while making a profit.
- Voluntary-run facilities are made up of inclusive and exclusive clubs that are non-profit making organisations. Volunteers give up their spare time to help run the club and facility, for no pay, although there may be a paid bar manager or facility manager.

A person's potential to make use of the provision available depends on many key variables:

- **Income**: public and voluntary sector provision tends to be more affordable than private provision.
- **Time available**: if a person is working or studying all the time they will struggle to have the time to make use of the provision available.
- **Motivation**: making use of the provision available requires a certain amount of motivation. Those who choose a sedentary lifestyle may find it hard to motivate themselves to leave the house and make use of the provision available.
- **Mobility**: if a person lacks the mobility to get to or make the most of the provision available, then they are less likely to attend.
- **Accessibility**: certain areas of the country have very little provision available. Those living in inner city areas tend to have more choice of provision available as there are more people to pay for memberships (private) and there is greater demand for public facilities. Voluntary sector provision depends entirely upon the availability of people to give up their free time to help run a facility or club. Many rural areas have very few facilities available.

> **Provision of sport**: how sport is provided by the public, private and voluntaries sectors.
>
> **Provision**: the act of providing or supplying something.

> **Exam tip**
>
> It is important you highlight many of the factors that affect provision and use of provision. The main factors can be remembered by using the acronym **TIMA**:
> - **T**ime available
> - **I**ncome
> - **M**obility and motivation
> - **A**ccessibility

> **Typical mistake**
>
> It is a mistake to suggest that all public sector facilities provide high quality facilities. They do sometimes, but private sector facilities tend to be of a higher quality.

Exam practice

1 Which of the following is a type of sporting provider? Tick one box only. [1]
- a public ☐
- b private ☐
- c voluntary ☐
- d all of the above ☐

2 Identify and explain one factor that affects a person's ability to make use of local sporting provision. [2]

3 Explain using examples why many children in Wales may find it difficult to access sporting provision. (WJEC only) [4]

ONLINE

> **Now test yourself**
>
> 1 What does provision mean?
> 2 What three sectors provide sporting facilities?
> 3 Name one factor that affects provision available.
>
> TESTED

Participation: factors that affect performance

The level of performance shown by any sports person is determined by a vast number of variables that are within and out of their control.

Controllable factors are those that the performer can influence or control. The extent of how much these affect the performer is determined by their **ability** to control or influence each factor. Controllable factors are shown in Table 5.1.

> **Controllable**: within the performer's control; they can affect the outcome.
>
> **Ability**: genetically inherited qualities to perform a task.
>
> **Uncontrollable**: out of the performer's control; they cannot affect the outcome.

Table 5.1. Controllable factors

Controllable factor	Explanation
Effort level	The level of effort that is put in by the performer is entirely down to them. The performer may well try hard on one occasion, then wish they had tried harder the next. Effort is also required for training.
Motivation	A performer must be motivated to do all 'the right things' including how to train, recover, eat, sleep, listen to advice, etc.
Psychological control	A performer must find ways to control their psychological state, including their arousal and emotions. Performers must show determination without direct aggression or breaking the rules.
Tactics and strategies	A performer can control the tactics and strategies that they use within their physical activity.
Diet and nutrition	A performer can control what they eat and drink in preparation for an event and during recovery.
Skill level	Skills can be learned and refined so a performer can work hard to improve their level of skill.

The **uncontrollable** factors in Table 5.2 do not allow the performer to directly have any influence.

Table 5.2 Uncontrollable factors

Uncontrollable factor	Explanation
Environment	A performer cannot control the surface, weather conditions or environmental factors in which they are competing.
Ability	Ability is inherited and is something you are born with. It cannot be directly controlled.
Opposition	A performer has no direct control over the ability level or performance of those opposing them in competition.
Referees and umpires	A performer cannot control decisions made by officials.
Access to provision	A performer cannot control what is available to them in terms of sporting provision. Where they live can be a barrier to performance due to a lack of facilities.
Luck	No one can prove if it actually exists, but a performer has no control over the level of luck.

Remember that the factors affecting provision, participation and performance can be interlinked. Thus, if there is no provision for an activity, it would negatively affect someone's ability to participate and their performance level is likely to be poor, if possible at all.

Choose one activity that you participate in regularly.

Write down:
- what provision there is locally for that activity
- two factors that have affected why you have participated in that activity
- two factors that have directly affected your performance level in that activity.

It is a common error to suggest that you can improve your ability. Ability does affect performance level, but it is inherited.

Now test yourself

TESTED ☐

1 Name one controllable factor that affects performance.
2 Name one uncontrollable factor that affects performance.
3 State what an ability is.

Exam practice

1 Which of the following is a controllable factor that affects performance level? Tick one box only. [1]
   a effort ☐
   b opponents ☐
   c environment ☐
   d referee ☐
2 Identify and explain two uncontrollable factors that affect the level of performance produced by an athlete. [2]
3 John is a long jumper who is not performing very well. He states that he is 'not very good and is therefore not trying hard'. Analyse his comments and justify whether they affect his performance level. [4]

ONLINE ☐

Participation: personal experiences that impact upon participation

REVISED

A person's choice of physical activity or sport can be influenced by a great number of variables. Many of these variables can be deemed to be personal experiences, as shown in Table 5.3.

Table 5.3 Influences on physical activity or sport

Personal experience	Influence
Past success	Performers are more likely to want to continue doing a sport or activity if they achieve some form of success. Success instills confidence and makes the performer comfortable with the demands of that activity.
Emotions	Performers will experience emotions when they try a sport or think about an activity. If that emotion is positive, they are more likely to want to try that activity again. If they fear something or do not think they would enjoy it, e.g. it was too physical for them, they are less likely to attend.
Feedback	If a performer receives feedback from a coach, parent or peer, the detail within the feedback can significantly influence their future choice of activity. For example, beginners tend to respond better to positive feedback than to negative feedback as negative may harm their confidence.
Coaching	The coach who introduces a performer to a sport can influence their future choice of activity. Positive, knowledgeable coaches who help performers to improve are more likely to encourage them to continue to attend compared to a coach who is negative and lacking in knowledge.
Facilities	Performers can be encouraged to take part in an activity if they have access to high quality facilities that are not available in other parts of the country.
Schooling	The school PE curriculum and the teachers teaching it can strongly influence what a person decides to take part in. Sometimes it depends what the school staff provide in terms of extra-curricular clubs.
Peers	A person's peers can influence their choice of activity. If they attend a club that their friends also attend, they are more likely to continue participating as they enjoy the social interaction as much as the sport. Performers may also see a peer perform well and gain confidence that they could also replicate their performance.
Family	Family perception and attitude can affect a person's choice of activity. If a performer mentions an activity at home, and receives a negative reply, they are less likely to continue that activity (and vice versa).
Culture/religion	As a person understands their culture and religion more as they mature, they may well understand that certain activities and sports are deemed more acceptable than others for their cultural/religious circumstances.

Exam practice

1 Outline **three** different personal experiences that may affect a person's choice of physical activity or sport. (Eduqas only) [3]
2 Give two possible reasons why a person might choose not to take part in a sport when there are high quality sports facilities in their local area. [2]
3 Evaluate the impact of experiences and provision on a person's choice of physical activity or sport. [2]

ONLINE

Now test yourself

1 Name a personal experience that can influence which activity you take part in.
2 What is meant by the term 'peers'?

TESTED

Participation: the influence of a school PE programme, extra-curricular and wider curriculum

All school children up to the age of 16 participate in physical education at school, as this is a compulsory part of their schooling. It is often when children leave school that many drop out of physical activity and sport. This makes it even more important that school PE programmes and the teachers delivering the content positively encourage the children to participate.

> **Curriculum PE**: the compulsory PE programme that is set by the government.
>
> **Extra-curricular PE**: extra clubs and opportunities that are outside of normal curricular PE.
>
> **Wider curriculum**: this curriculum, which is not compulsory, can include opportunities to play sport, dance, attend extra art, and so on.

A person's schooling can play a very important part in influencing what they decide to take part in. A school that offers particular activities is more likely to encourage larger numbers to continue with that activity after they have left school. The provision of **curriculum PE**, **extra-curricular** activities and the **wider curriculum** is shown in Table 5.4.

Exam tip

The clue is in the name:
- **C**urriculum is **c**ompulsory.
- **Extra**-curricular is **extra** to the curriculum.
- **Wider** curriculum involves the **wider** parts of the school.

Revision activity

Write down the words:
- Curriculum
- Extra
- Wider

... and outline what your school offers in terms of all three to encourage participation.

Table 5.4 School provision

Aspect of school	What it is	How it affects performers
Curriculum PE	Curriculum PE is the compulsory programme that all students must follow, delivered by professional PE teachers.	All children experience certain activities. All children are taught by a professionally qualified teacher.
Extra-curricular PE	Extra-curricular opportunities are the clubs and activities that are offered to students outside of curriculum PE time. These opportunities are voluntary.	The clubs available are dependent on what the school wants to offer. Delivered by PE teachers or external coaches or volunteers. This allows children to further develop an activity they choose to pursue.
Wider curriculum	This involves all opportunities outside of the compulsory curriculum, e.g. sport, art, dance, music, etc. The wider curriculum can involve cross-curricular links.	The main aspects taught in PE can be reinforced in other areas of the school. Encourages aspects of healthy living for life. Often known as developing healthy habits.

Exam practice

1 Describe the difference between 'curriculum PE' and the 'wider curriculum'. [2]
2 Explain how curriculum PE can influence the choice/s of physical activity and sport for school children. [2]
3 Evaluate the use of extra-curricular PE in encouraging children to take part in sporting activities for life. [4]

ONLINE

Now test yourself

1 What is curriculum PE?
2 What is extra-curricular PE?
3 What is the 'wider curriculum'?

TESTED

Participation: physical literacy, physical activity, health and well-being

REVISED

It is generally deemed important that children learn, develop and adopt a desire to take part in physical activity and exercise.

Physical Education lessons at school start to inform children about many concepts and ideas. However, the government aims for children to mature and develop a 'sporting habit for life', a stated aim of the Department for Culture, Media and Sport. In developing a desire to take part in activity, the government also aims to develop the **physical literacy** of children. This is a concept that enables people to build a sense of purpose, confidence and motivation to take part in activity. It is a really important feature that should enable young people to learn how to include regular activity in a purposeful manner in their lives.

The idea is that young people should want to take part in and appreciate the benefits that activity brings, including widening their view of the world, and to learn what they can do and could achieve. As physical literacy grows, so does a person's confidence and motivation to try out new activities, as they know they will be able to take part successfully. The obvious benefit of taking part in physical activity is an increase in health and well-being (as detailed on page 44).

Physical literacy: described as the motivation, confidence, physical competence, knowledge and understanding to value and take responsibility for engagement in physical activities for life.

Exam tip

Try to remember the link: physical activity → increases physical literacy → increases a child's likelihood of developing a sporting habit for life.

Typical mistake

It is a common mistake to think that physical literacy is to do with writing words related to sport.

Revision activity

Try to create a flow diagram with the words 'Physical activity' at the top. Then draw arrows down and write down positive effects of taking part in physical activity (including physical literacy).

Figure 5.1 Benefits of taking part in physical activity

Now test yourself

TESTED

1 What is physical activity?
2 What is physical literacy?
3 What does 'sporting habit for life' mean?

Exam practice

1 Identify **three** positive effects of developing a child's physical literacy. [3]
2 Explain how the development of physical literacy can affect the three components of health and well-being. [3]
3 Evaluate the impact of providing opportunities for children to experience physical activity from an early age. [4]

ONLINE

Strategies to improve participation

In order to address the barriers to participation that many groups face, the government and various sporting bodies administer policies and campaigns to target specific types of people.

The Creating an Active Wales programme aims to seek to ensure that issues of diversity are considered in the development and delivery of its actions. Its policy aims to ensure that no group is disadvantaged and that targeted interventions may be required to ensure this is the case.

'Climbing Higher'

Climbing Higher (2006) is the Welsh Assembly Government's twenty-year policy to increase participation rates of people in Wales. The funding will target specific 'audiences' such as teenagers, young adults leaving education, those from areas of multiple deprivation, women and girls generally, those from ethnic minorities and those with disabilities.

'This Girl Can'

The 'This Girl Can' campaign aims to celebrate active women who are exercising, no matter how well they do it, or how they look. The campaign aims to help women overcome the fear of judgement that is stopping too many women and girls from joining in.

'What Moves You?'

'What Moves You' is a campaign to get the women of Wales to dig out their trainers and fall in love with sport. It is administered by Sport Wales and acknowledges that not all women perceive the idea of exercising as something positive.

'Kick It Out'

'Let's Kick **Racism** Out of Football' was launched in 1993 by the Commission for Racial Equality and the Professional Football Association (PFA). The campaign has changed its name after many years and is now known as 'Kick It Out'. Its aim is to tackle **discrimination** in football.

'Together We Will'

'The Together We Will' campaign aims to increase the number of people with disabilities who regularly take part in sport or exercise. Some key findings of the Active People Survey show that people with disabilities:

● sometimes do not find opportunities accessible or appealing
● do not know where to find out information
● are often looking to have fun, sometimes with able-bodied people.

Eight National Disability Sports Organisations (NDSOs) are working with the English Federation of Disability Sport to deliver the campaign, with backing from Sport England.

Racism: prejudice or discrimination against a particular group based on race.

Now test yourself

1 What is meant by racism?
2 Name a campaign that aims to increase participation of all groups.
3 Name a campaign that targets one specific group.

TESTED

Exam practice

1 Which of the following is **not** a campaign that includes an aim to encourage participation among women? Tick **one** box only. [1]
   a This Girl Can
   b What Moves You?
   c Kick It Out
   d Climbing Higher
2 Identify and explain one campaign that exists in Wales to target a specific group of people to increase participation rates in sporting activity. (WJEC only) [3]

ONLINE

Provision

For many years, the government has tried to encourage participation in all groups within society. Strategies to increase participation rates have been put in place to address barriers that prevent these groups from participating in higher numbers. The barriers and strategies are outlined in Table 5.5.

Table 5.5 Barriers and strategies to increase participation in sport and physical activity

Target group	Provision and barriers	Strategies to increases participation of target group
Women	● Affected by **stereotypical sexist** views of what women should do ● Some sports are still male-dominated ● Lack of provision to play certain sports ● Less media coverage given to female performers ● Fewer female role models	● Female–only classes/clubs ● Campaigns to encourage participation, e.g. 'This Girl Can' ● Increase in coverage on TV, e.g. women's football ● Encourage positive female role models in sport ● Provision of crèche facilities in leisure centres
People with disabilities	● Performers with **disabilities** face access issues with certain facilities ● Lack of specialist clubs ● Lack of specialist coaches ● Few role models ● Lack of media coverage	● Adapted facilities to enable access ● Adapted activities, e.g. wheelchair basketball ● Campaigns to encourage participation, e.g. 'Together We Will' ● Specialist clubs for performers with disabilities and some integrated activities mixing able and less able ● Develop specialist coaches ● Promote positive role models from disabled sport, e.g. Paralympics ● Increase media coverage of events, e.g. Paralympics
Race/ethnic minorities	● Some cultures/religions have clothing restrictions ● Religious holidays can affect sports participation ● Often not seen as the cultural norm to play certain sports ● Few role models or coaches from specific cultures/races ● Under-representation of ethnic minorities in most sports ● Elements of racism still exist in sport	● Specific campaigns to target ethnic minority groups, e.g. Sporting Equals ● Promote role models from culturally diverse backgrounds ● Provide opportunities for coaches to progress from ethnic minorities ● Campaigns to eradicate racism in sport, e.g. Kick It Out

Disability: physical or mental condition that affects a person's ability to move, use their senses or perform tasks or activities.

Discrimination: the unjust or prejudicial treatment of different categories of people, especially on the grounds of race, age or sex.

Prejudice: preconceived opinion about a person or group of people.

Sexism: prejudice, stereotyping or discrimination based on a person's gender.

Stereotype: a widely held but fixed and oversimplified image or idea of a particular type of person or thing.

Now test yourself

1 What is meant by discrimination?
2 What is meant by sexism?
3 Name some common strategies that are designed to affect the participation rates of certain groups.

TESTED

Exam practice

1 Identify and explain potential strategies to increase participation rates among members of the population with disabilities. [4]

ONLINE

Exam practice and Data analysis answers at **www.hoddereducation.co.uk/myrevisionnotes**

Performance: commercialisation

Commercialisation is deemed to be the process of introducing products that can be bought or sold for money into the marketplace. The world of sport is undoubtedly a 'sector' where there are many opportunities to sell merchandise and products to the watching public. Every aspect of sport can be deemed a commodity that can be bought and sold. For example:

- Players can be bought and sold.
- Sports clothing can be bought and sold.
- Sports equipment can be bought and sold.
- Sports stadia can be bought and sold.
- The **media** can buy the rights to televise sport.
- **Sponsorship** of an event can be bought.
- Tickets can be bought and sold, and so on.

The world of sport is inevitably linked to the media and subsequently to the watching spectators. The link also includes sponsors who aim to market their company. This overall link is called the **golden triangle**.

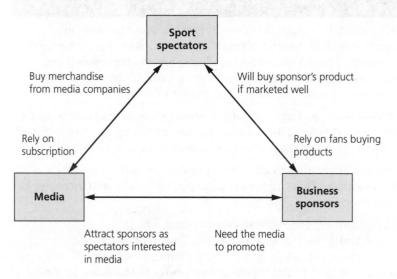

Figure 5.2 The golden triangle

The golden triangle involves a continuous cycle of links between sports fans, sponsors and the media. A company may decide to sponsor an event to develop 'brand awareness' and possibly encourage the watching public to buy their products. As products and names are advertised through sponsorship, these names are seen in the media coverage of the sport. As a result, watching fans may well decide to buy merchandise or products.

> **Commercialisation**: the process of introducing products that can be bought or sold for money into the marketplace
>
> **Media**: means of communication including social media, television, radio, newspapers, and so on.
>
> **Sponsorship**: paying to attach your company name to an event or person.
>
> **Golden triangle**: the financial relationship between sport, the media and spectators.

Exam tip

Don't forget that sport is inextricably linked to its fans, the media and sponsorship.

Typical mistake

It is a common error for students to suggest that the media is just television; it also includes newspapers, radio and social media.

Revision activity

Draw a triangle and try to turn that triangle into a representation of the golden triangle.

Exam practice

1 Which of the following is not a part of the 'golden triangle'? Tick **one** box only. [1]
   a spectators ☐
   b sponsors ☐
   c media ☐
   d sports officials ☐
2 Explain the role of spectators within the 'golden triangle'. [2]
3 Evaluate the benefit of commercialisation to a sponsor. [4]

ONLINE

Now test yourself

1 What is commercialisation?
2 What is the media?
3 What is sponsorship?
4 What is the golden triangle?

TESTED

Performance: links between media and commercialisation

REVISED

The golden triangle shows the relationship between sports spectators, sponsors and the media. The media's role in commercialised activity is key as, without the exposure through the media, sponsors would not be able to advertise the products and brand names.

Sponsorship brings vast amounts of money to sport and allows a sponsor to:
- gain publicity and **brand exposure** and awareness
- associate themselves with an athlete or team
- support the local community or particular individuals
- gain benefits in their tax calculations.

Sponsors rely on the media to show their name and/or brands. As a result, the media may help sponsors indirectly, as shown in Table 5.6.

Social media: computer-based technology allowing the sharing of social information, for example Twitter, Facebook and so on.

Brand exposure: making the brand name of a product or company better known to consumers.

Table 5.6 How the media can help sponsors

Media	Role for the sponsor
Television	Television provides a visual image of the sport. Coverage of sport is now extensive and allows viewers to see the sport and all of the advertising that is included in sport. As a result, viewers may become more aware of brand names and products, e.g. football advertising is now electronic and allows moving pictures to be shown during games. Commercialised activity may well increase as viewers purchase advertised brands or products.
Newspapers	If an event is sponsored, e.g. Heineken Cup Rugby, pictures in the newspaper may well show the branding of Heineken and articles will refer to the event as the 'Heineken Cup'. Commercialised activity may well increase as readers purchase the advertised brand or products.
Radio	If an event is sponsored, e.g. Heineken Cup Rugby, radio presenters will refer to the event using its full name, e.g. 'the Heineken Cup'. Commercialised activity may well increase as listeners purchase the advertised brand or products.
Social media	The use of **social media** has grown exponentially in recent years. The use of a hashtag (#) allows specific words to trend and/or be tracked via Twitter. Thus if an event like the Heineken Cup is trending on Twitter, Heineken as a brand gets more exposure. If an event is sponsored, e.g. Heineken Cup Rugby, social media use will refer to the event as the 'Heineken Cup'. Commercialised activity may well increase as social media users purchase the advertised brand or products.

Typical mistake

It is a common error to assume that TV directly increases the sales of products. It does this indirectly as TV simply broadcasts the event. It is the fact that sponsors' names can be seen/heard at the event via the media that increases commercialised activity.

Now test yourself

1 What is social media?
2 What is brand exposure?

TESTED

Exam practice

1 Which of the following are forms of media? Tick **one** box only. [1]
   a television ☐
   b radio ☐
   c newspapers ☐
   d all of the above ☐
2 Explain the role of social media in potentially increasing commercialised activity. [3]

ONLINE

Revision activity

Start a flow chart with the word 'Sponsor' at the top. Try to recreate the links between a sponsor and a consumer, outlining the role of media coverage.

Exam practice and Data analysis answers at **www.hoddereducation.co.uk/myrevisionnotes**

Performance: gamesmanship

Gamesmanship is the use of controversial methods to win or gain an advantage in a physical activity or sport. However, these methods are not technically illegal or against the rules.

Forms of gamesmanship are often referred to as 'pushing the rules to the limit without getting caught' and can involve using dubious methods to achieve the desired result.

Examples of gamesmanship that are often used in sport include:
- time-wasting in hockey by hitting the ball out of play
- slow play in golf
- smashing a ball (tennis) or shuttlecock (badminton) at the opponent
- golf match play – not conceding a small putt
- sledging (putting the batsmen off) in cricket
- taking a toilet break in tennis when it is not actually needed
- taking a very long time to serve in a racket sport to unsettle the opponent.

Figure 5.3 Taking a long time to serve in badminton would be using gamesmanship to unsettle an opponent

There are a large number of reasons why performers use gamesmanship. Examples include:
- pressure to win from sponsors/coach/crowd/media
- importance of the event
- it has become quite normal to use gamesmanship
- low level of sportsmanship
- previous history of opponent/s using gamesmanship
- win at all costs attitude.

> **Gamesmanship**: the use of controversial methods to gain an advantage or to win that push the boundaries/rules to their limit.

> **Exam tip**
>
> Try to ensure you have at least two different examples of gamesmanship from two different sports in preparation for the examination.

> **Typical mistake**
>
> It is a common mistake to confuse gamesmanship with deviance. Deviance is outside of the rules. Gamesmanship is within the rules but pushes them to the limits.

> **Revision activity**
>
> Write down five different sports and five different ways that performers can use acts of gamesmanship to gain an advantage.

Now test yourself

TESTED ☐

1 What is gamesmanship?
2 Give one example of gamesmanship.

Exam practice

1 Explain how gamesmanship may be used in a team sport of your choice. [2]
2 A performer is grunting in tennis when serving. The opponent complains to the umpire. Is this a form of gamesmanship? Justify your answer. [3]

ONLINE ☐

Performance: gamesmanship

Performance: sportsmanship

In all sport, there is an unwritten expectation that sports people will abide by the rules and play 'fairly'. The act of being 'sporting' and showing **sportsmanship** tends to involve polite, fair behaviour that is respectful of an opponent or opponents. Showing sportsmanship involves following the **etiquette** of the sport – the unwritten rules regarding behaviour.

Sporting behaviour can be seen in nearly every sport. Media coverage puts a spotlight on sports people and they are expected to show the behaviour of a positive role model. Subsequently, the intention is that all levels of sports people, having been inspired by their role model, will show similar behaviour.

> **Sportsmanship:** behaviour that is appropriate, fair, polite and respectful. It is often called 'fair play'.
>
> **Etiquette:** unwritten rules regarding behaviour.

Table 5.7 Examples of sportsmanship in different sports

Sport	Example of sportsmanship
Football	Shaking the hands of the opposition before or after the match
Rugby	Creating a tunnel to clap your opponents off the field
Golf	Not walking across the line of an opponent's putt
Tennis	Before serving it is sporting to wait to see if the opponent on the other side of the net is ready to receive the serve
Football	Having conceding a free kick in football, the defending team should retreat 10 yards behind the football when the free kick is taken
Athletics	If a performer is being 'lapped' in a long running race, it is sporting to move out of the way of the runner who is overtaking
Netball	It is sporting behaviour to clap when the opposition score

The relationship between the media, sportsmanship and role models can be seen in Figure 5.4.

Now test yourself

1 What is sportsmanship?
2 What is etiquette?
3 Give an example of sportsmanship.

TESTED

Exam practice

1 Describe what is meant by the term sportsmanship and identify **two** different examples of how this concept is shown in sport. [3]
2 A performer pokes another player in the eye during a rugby scrum. Is this an example of bad sportsmanship or gamesmanship? Justify your answer. [3]

ONLINE

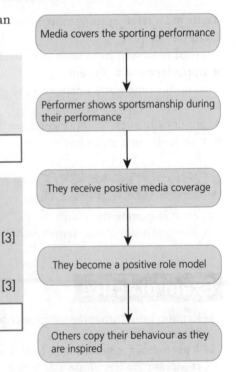

Media covers the sporting performance

↓

Performer shows sportsmanship during their performance

↓

They receive positive media coverage

↓

They become a positive role model

↓

Others copy their behaviour as they are inspired

Figure 5.4 The relationship between the media, sportsmanship and role models

Performance: deviance

Deviance is the act of doing something that can be seen as drifting away from the norms of conventional behaviour. However, deviance can be positive or negative.

- **Negative deviance** in sport is behaviour outside the norms or rules of the sport. Taking illegal performance-enhancing drugs, is an example of negative deviance.
- **Positive deviance** is behaviour outside the norms but not against the rules, for example, training too hard or continuing to play when injured. It can be argued that much of the deviance that occurs in modern day sport is due to pressure from spectators, the media and sponsors.

Negative deviance comes in many forms but is not always easy to see. If a performer has taken illegal performance-enhancing drugs, they are only detectable via a suitable drug test. Similarly, if a performer has played a part in illegal betting or match fixing, this may not be easy to detect while they are playing.

Other more obvious forms of negative deviance include deliberate acts that break the rules, for example, deliberately fouling a player or trying to gain an advantage by using an illegal technique or manipulating equipment. Examples of this include:

- ball-tampering in cricket
- deliberate handball in football
- high tackle in rugby.

Positive deviance is to do with over-conforming. This means that the performer may well train when injured or continue to play or compete when injured. This is not 'normal' behaviour as such but may have arisen due to excessive pressure from an external source: crowd, coach, sponsor, media attention, and so on.

> **Deviance:** behaviour that is outside of the norms of the sport.

Typical mistake

Students often forget the idea of positive deviance. Students also commonly forget the difference between gamesmanship and deviance. Deviance is generally against the rules, whereas gamesmanship is not.

Now test yourself

TESTED

1 What is positive deviance?
2 What is negative deviance?
3 Give an example of each.

Exam tip

Go into your exam with at least two examples of negative deviance and one example of positive deviance.

Exam practice

1 Explain, using an example, what is meant by the term 'negative deviance'. [2]
2 Give **three** reasons why a hockey player may continue to play the last 15 minutes of a game even though they are injured. [3]

ONLINE

Revision activity

Write down three different physical activities and ways for each in which a performer could act in a deviant manner (negatively and positively).

Premier League example

Table 5.8 shows the football teams in the Premier League with the ten best disciplinary records from the 2016–17 season.

1 How many teams did not receive a red card during the whole of the season? [1]

2 Based on the information provided, which team appears to have committed most negative deviant acts? [1]

3 Suggest what deviant acts this team may have committed. [2]

4 As Liverpool finished top of the 'fair play league', describe the relationship between the sportsmanship they may have shown and the media coverage of their season. [4]

5 Explain the difference between gamesmanship, sportsmanship and negative deviance. [3]

Table 5.8 **Premier League fair play table**

Team	Yellows	Reds	Points
1 Liverpool	54	0	216
2 Swansea	56	0	224
3 Bournemouth	52	3	240
4 Tottenham	62	0	248
5 Southampton	59	2	256
6 Burnley	65	2	282
7 Chelsea	72	0	288
8 Leicester	72	1	300
9 Stoke City	70	2	302
10 Crystal Palace	77	0	308

Participation example

The data included in the bar chart (Figure 5.5) identify how often people were playing sport in England in 2005–06 compared to 2014–15.

How often people are playing sport

Try to answer the following questions:

1 In what time period were the most people playing sport at least three times a week?

2 State what happened between 2005–06 and 2014–15 with regards to:
   a taking part at least once a month
   b taking part at least once a week
   c taking part at least twice a week
   d taking part at least three times a week.

3 As the population of England totals approximately 55 million, account for the large number of people who do not take part in physical activity. [6]

4 Sport Wales report that the number of adults hooked on sport – participating three times a week or more – in Wales is up 41 per cent according to the official Active Adults Survey. Suggest reasons for this increase. [4]

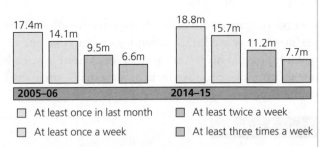

2005–06	2014–15
17.4m 14.1m 9.5m 6.6m	18.8m 15.7m 11.2m 7.7m

☐ At least once in last month   ▨ At least twice a week

☐ At least once a week   ▨ At least three times a week

Source: Active People Survey 1 and Active People Survey 9 (Sport England 2005–06 and 2014–15)

Figure 5.5 **Bar charts to show number of adults taking part in sport at moderate intensity by frequency**

Data analysis tools

It is important that you can show an understanding of the types of data that can be collected. Data is basically divided into two types:
- quantitative data
- qualitative data.

Quantitative data

Quantitative data deals with numbers or, in other words, deals with quantities.

Quantitative data is a measurement that can be quantified as a number, for example, time in seconds or baskets scored in basketball. There is no opinion involved; it is factual, numerical information.

There are many areas of the specification that could be used to represent quantitative data, for example:
- fitness tests produce numerical scores
- heart rate is measured in beats per minute and can therefore be plotted on a graph
- engagement patterns of women, people with disabilities and ethnic minorities.

Qualitative data

Qualitative data comes from opinions. It is subjective as it allows for different people to express a viewpoint.

Qualitative statements involve a person's opinions relating to the quality of a performance rather than the quantity. A fitness test could produce a numerical score (quantitative), but the person carrying out the test may well suggest that they 'did really well'. This would be a qualitative opinion.

Most topics within the specification can be examined through questions that refer to qualitative data. For example:
- the opinions expressed about the positive or negative impact of commercialisation
- the opinions expressed about the value of extrinsic rewards.

Quantitative data: data that can be quantified as a number, for example, time in seconds or goals scored. There is no opinion expressed (qualitative). It is a fact.

Qualitative data: data that is subjective, involving opinions relating to the quality of a performance rather than the quantity.

Understanding how data is collected

Quantitative data involving quantities and amounts tends to be gathered using the following methods:
- **Questionnaires**: a series of questions where the number of people who give a certain answer can be expressed as a quantity.
- **Surveys**: for example, in the television programme 'Family Fortunes', the host uses the number of people who expressed a particular answer!

However, with specific reference to Physical Education, it is also likely that other data collection could be used. For example:
- heart rate monitors to measure heart rate
- stopwatches to gain a time, for example, in the Illinois agility test
- metre ruler to gain a score, for example, in the reaction time test.

Qualitative data involving opinions is generally gathered through the following methods:
- interviews
- observations.

With specific reference to Physical Education, you may well see from an observation that a performer appears to be motivated, or interview a participant after a fitness test who expresses their delight at their score.

Exam tip

Remember:
- **quantit**ative = **quantity**
- **qualit**ative = **quality**.

Now test yourself answers

1 Health, training and exercise

Health, fitness and well-being

1 Physical, mental and social.
2 Fitness enables a person to carry out their everyday life and job without fatigue.

The contribution that physical activity makes to health and fitness

1 Being well enough to take part in physical activity.
2 Feeling confident enough to take part in physical activity.
3 Feeling confident in socialising with people when taking part in physical activity.

Consequences of a sedentary lifestyle

1 The choice to take part in little or no activity.
2 Because a person is uneducated or ill-informed etc.

Diet and nutrition

1 Energy at all intensities.
2 Energy at a low intensity.
3 Growth and repair.

Components of fitness

1 Changing direction at speed.
2 Supplying oxygen to the working muscles.
3 During, for example, a 100m sprint

Measuring health and fitness (1)

1 To identify strengths and weaknesses, and to identify areas to be improved through a training programme.
2 Examples include the Illinois agility test for agility, and the multi-stage fitness test for cardiovascular endurance.

Measuring health and fitness (2)

1 Repeating a test and getting similar results.
2 When a test actually tests what it states that it will test.
3 How a test is carried out.

Methods: interval training

1 Exercising for a sustained period of time without rest at steady state intensity.
2 Training method that incorporates periods of work interspersed with periods of rest.
3 Swedish name for 'speed play' whereby the work rate intensity and terrain change from high to lower and back to higher.

Methods: plyometrics

1 The use of body weight to initiate an eccentric contraction which causes a concentric contraction.
2 Eccentric contractions are lengthening, concentric contractions are shortening.

Methods: weight training

1 One complete lift of the weight.
2 A group of several repetitions.
3 The maximum weight that can safely be lifted in one repetition.

Methods: flexibility training

1 A held stretch.
2 A moving stretch.
3 A partner-assisted stretch.
4 A stretch in which the agonist holds the stretch.

Principles of training and exercising (1)

1 Specificity, progression, overload, variance.
2 Frequency, intensity, duration.

Principles of training and exercising (2)

1 80+ per cent of 1-rep max.
2 60–80 per cent of max heart rate.
3 Health.

Warming up

1 Three.
2 Pulse raiser.
3 In the final part of the warm-up.

Cooling down

1 Three.
2 Yes.
3 **D**elayed **O**nset of **M**uscle **S**oreness.

2 Exercise physiology

Structure of the skeletal system

1 Hinge.
2 Ball and socket.
3 Ball and socket.
4 Hinge.

Function of the skeletal system

1 Bending/closing the angle.
2 Opening the angle at a joint.
3 Moving away from the body.
4 Moving towards the midline of the body.
5 Flexion/extension.

Structure of the muscular system

1 Muscle attached to skeleton to cause movement.
2 Muscle inside hollow organs to enable functions.
3 Muscle in wall of heart, involuntary muscle.

Muscle fibre types

1 Fast and slow.
2 Fast.
3 Slow.

Cardio-respiratory and vascular systems: structure

1 Blood flow between heart and body.
2 Blood flow between heart and lungs.
3 Atria and ventricles.

Cardio-respiratory and vascular systems: blood vessels

1 Vessel that carries blood away from the heart.
2 Vessel that carries blood back towards the heart.
3 Vessel allowing gas exchange.
4 – Arteries have a high pressure and carry oxygenated blood to the body.
   – Veins have a lower pressure and carry blood back to the heart to be oxygenated at the lungs.
   – Capillaries allow for gas exchange and removal of waste products.

Cardio-respiratory and vascular systems: functions of blood vessels

1 The opening up of arteries to allow more blood through.
2 The closing of arteries to let less blood through.
3 Via arteries.

Cardio-respiratory and vascular systems: cardiac values

1 The amount of blood ejected from the heart per minute.
2 60–90 bpm.
3 mmHg.

Cardio-respiratory and vascular systems: respiratory system

1 Tiny air sacs in the lungs which allow gas exchange.
2 Trachea, bronchi, bronchioles, alveoli, red blood cells in blood.
3 From an area of high concentration to low concentration.

Cardio-respiratory and vascular systems: lung volumes

1 Amount of air taken in or expired per breath.
2 It increases.
3 Minute volume = tidal volume x breaths per minute.

Aerobic and anaerobic exercise

1 Exercise occurring when there is enough oxygen to supply the energy required.
2 Exercise occurring when there is an insufficient amount of oxygen to supply energy.
3 When the oxygen supply is not meeting the demand and lactic acid starts to build up significantly.

The characteristics and factors affecting aerobic/anaerobic exercise

1 Aerobic is low-to-medium intensity and long duration.
2 Anaerobic is high intensity and low duration.
3 Aerobic exercise.

The role of nutrients in different intensities of exercise

1 Low intensity.
2 Low, medium and high.
3 To prevent dehydration.

Short-term effects of exercise

1 The cardiovascular system includes the heart, vessels and blood. The cardio-respiratory system is the cardiovascular system PLUS breathing mechanisms.
2 These include:
   - The skin may start to turn red as the blood flows closer to the surface.
   - Body temperature starts to increase.
   - Sweat may start to be produced in larger quantities.
   - Heart rate and breathing rate will start to increase.
3 Varying effects on:
   - the muscular system
   - the skeletal system
   - the cardiovascular system
   - the cardiorespiratory system
   - energy systems being used.

Long-term effects of exercise

1 Can increase lactic acid tolerance. Can use aerobic system at higher intensity.
2 Improved muscle tone and improved muscular endurance.
3 Increase in size.

Effects of exercise on health and well-being

1 For example, able to train regularly.
2 For example, feel positive about performing.
3 For example, meet new friends.

3 Movement analysis

Muscle contractions: isotonic and isometric

1 Muscle contracts and shortens.
2 Muscle contracts and lengthens.
3 Muscle holds its length during contraction.

Muscle contractions: antagonistic muscle action

1 The prime mover causing the action.
2 The pair of muscles that work as an opposite to each other – as one contracts, the other relaxes (and vice versa).

Lever systems

1 123, FLE.
2 Triceps extension at the elbow.
3 Ankle.
4 Flexion at elbow.

Planes and axes of movement: planes

1 Forwards or backwards movements.
2 Side to side movements.
3 Rotational movement/turning in certain ways.

Planes and axes of movement: axes

1 Movements in the transverse plane.
2 Movements in the sagittal plane.
3 Movements in the frontal plane.

Sports technology for the performer

1 For example, calorie reader, nutritional software.
2 For example, an ice bath.
3 For example, cameras, recordings.

Sports technology for the coach

1 For example, a heart rate monitor.
2 For example, an ice bath.
3 Positive: ensures the performer is suitably protected. Negative: can be time consuming.

Sports technology for the official

1 For example, goal line technology in football.
2 For example, football referees using intercom headsets.

4 Psychology of sport and physical activity

Goal-setting

1 A goal regarding the outcome only – e.g., to win.
2 A goal dealing with a performance aspect or technique.

Goal-setting: SMART targets

1 Specific, Measureable, Agreed, Realistic and Time-phased.
2 Being specific to the demands of the sport, movements and muscles used.

Information processing (1)

1 Via the senses/display.
2 A filtering system – concentrating on the most important cues in the display and filtering out the irrelevant ones.
3 Short- and long-term memory.

Information processing (2)

1 Feedback that comes from another person.
2 Feedback that comes from oneself.

3 Feedback that is based on technique and performance.

4 Feedback that is based on the outcome or result.

Guidance

1 Guidance that is heard.

2 Guidance that is seen.

3 Being physically moved.

4 Being helped by an object/aid.

Mental preparation

1 Imagining a calming environment to reduce tension and arousal. It can be imaging the feeling of a movement or watching a recording of your own movement.

2 Picturing the perfect performance.

Motivation

1 The drive to succeed or the desire to want to achieve something.

2 The drive that comes from within oneself, e.g., for pride.

3 The drive experienced by a performer when aiming to win a tangible or intangible reward.

Characteristics of a skilled performance

1 Technically sound/ effective/ accurate/ consistent/ fluent/ efficient.

2 Technically sound/ effective/ accurate/ consistent/ fluent/ efficient.

3 Physical.

Classification of skills

1 Whether the environment is stable or not.

2 Depends on the simplicity and number of decisions to be made.

3 Whether the performance is done in performer's own time or controlled by an external factor.

Types of practice

1 The whole skill practised without breaks.

2 Parts of the skill practised separately.

3 The same skill practised in the same way over and over.

4 A skill practised in changing environments or with changing demands.

Classification of skills and types of practice: applications

1 Part.

2 Whole.

3 Fixed.

5 Socio-cultural issues in sport and physical activity

Participation: factors that affect participation

1 For example, gender or role models.

2 **G**ender, **R**ole models, **A**ccess, **F**amily and friends, **T**ime and income.

Participation: factors affecting provision

1 Access to and facilities available for sport.

2 Public, private and voluntary.

3 For example, time or money available.

Participation: factors that affect performance

1 For example, effort, motivation, skill.

2 For example, opposition, referee, ability.

3 An ability is a genetically inherited quality to perform a task.

Participation: personal experiences that impact upon participation

1 For example, peers, family, success, coach, emotions.

2 Friends.

Participation: the influence of a school PE programme, extra-curricular and wider curriculum

1 The compulsory PE programme, which is set by the government.

2 Extra clubs and opportunities that are outside of normal curricular PE.

3 The curriculum that is not compulsory but can include opportunities to play sport, dance, attend extra art, etc.

Participation: physical literacy, physical activity, health and well-being

1 Any form of exercise/sport/recreation.

2 The motivation, confidence, physical competence, knowledge and understanding to value and take responsibility for engagement in physical activities for life.

3 Developing a desire to take part in physical activities for the whole of one's life.

Strategies to improve participation

1 Prejudice or discrimination against a particular group based on race.

2 For example, Climbing Higher.

3 For example, What Moves You (women).

Provision

1 The unjust or prejudicial treatment of different categories of people, especially on the grounds of race, age, or sex.

2 Prejudice, stereotyping or discrimination based on a person's gender.

3 For example, campaigns, role models, specialist clubs.

Performance: commercialisation

1 The process of introducing products into the market place that can be bought or sold for money.

2 Means of communication including social media, television, radio, newspapers, etc.

3 Paying to attach your company name to an event or person.

4 The financial relationship between sport, the media and spectators.

Performance: links between media and commercialisation

1 Computer-based technology allowing the sharing of social information, for example, Twitter and Facebook.

2 Making the brand name of a product or company better known to consumers.

Performance: gamesmanship

1 Bending the rules to gain an advantage.

2 For example, time wasting.

Performance: sportsmanship

1 Behaviour that is appropriate, fair, polite and respectful. Often called 'fair play'.

2 Unwritten rules regarding behaviour.

3 For example, shaking hands at the end of a match.

Performance: deviance

1 Over-conforming to the norms.

2 Behaviour which is deemed to be outside of the rules.

3 Positive: training when injured.

Negative: drug taking.